COMMENTS O

"I was very, very impressed . . . so impresses me is WHAT Honstadt is saying . . . how clearly, succinctly, and boldly he's saying it . . . and how much it needs to be heard. Hohstadt brings a career as a symphony conductor to the challenges facing the church. His artistic sensitivity, his intuitive reach into the unknown, his fascinating quotations, and his energetic writing style combine to make this a book well worth reading and recommending to others. If we listen to him, we'll make more beautiful music in the years ahead." **Brian McLaren, Author, *Reinventing Your Church***

"Forget the future. This is a book for the 'now'. Hohstadt is neither afraid to speak prophetically nor prone to 'analysis lite'. His fascinating guide to 'prophetic metaphor' is, in and of itself, worth the price of admission." **Sally Morgenthaler, Author, *Worship Evangelism***

"Dying to Live: The 21st Century Church will inspire you as well as provoke you to think. Thomas Hohstadt looks forward and speaks the essence of what the future may unfold and how the Church will relate to it. This book will help you analyze and re-evaluate your effectiveness in reaching the new culture of the Digital Age." **LaMar Boschman, The Worship Institute**

"This is a thought-provoking analysis of how our paradigms of worship are of necessity going to be changing in today's accelerating world. 'Dying to Live' will give you an insightful peek into the landscape that awaits us, and for which we must prepare." **Bob Sorge, Author, *Exploring Worship***

"It is on target . . . it has passion and conviction, and it is on a theme that is timely . . . Hohstadt is onto important ideas." **Loren B. Mead, The Alban Institute; Author, *The Once and Future Church***

"Powerful . . . Extraordinary . . . Stimulating . . . His images and prophetic tone are very strong." **Rex Miller, Strategic Planner and Futurist**

"It grows on you, as it strips away unnessary thoughts, it reveals what is often concealed; it explodes certain concepts, while revealing the true truth. . . . There were points of brilliance . . . I am happy as well as honoured to read *Dying to Live.*" **Joel Young, Author, *Behold Yeshua!***

"An interesting and provocative book on an important subject." **Richard Cimino, Editor, *Religion Watch***

"Powerhouse . . . true revelation . . . a refreshing clarity of language." **Ed Chinn, Writer and Organizational Consultant**

DYING TO LIVE

THE 21st CENTURY CHURCH

By

Thomas Hohstadt

"Except a corn of wheat fall into the ground and die, it abideth alone: but if it die, it bringeth forth much fruit." John 12:24

Damah Media
3522 Maple Street
Odessa, Texas 79762
915/366-0457

DYING TO LIVE: THE 21ST CENTURY CHURCH
by Thomas Hohstadt

ISBN 0-937383-18-X

First Printing, 1999

Printed in the United States of America

Dedicated to

LaMar and Rex

who made it possible

TABLE OF CONTENTS

FOREWORD ix

I. INTRODUCTION 1
   1. APOCALYPTIC VISIONS 1
   2. HOW WE GOT HERE 13
   3. . . . WHERE WE'RE GOING 25

II. THE PROMISE 37
   4. "EXCEEDINGLY GREAT PROMISES" 37
   5. "ONCE MORE WITH FEELING" 49

III. THE IMPERATIVE 62
   6. EATING ELEPHANTS 62
   7. DYING TO LIVE 68
   8. TURNING THE CHURCH UPSIDE-DOWN 73
   9. CROSSING FORBIDDEN BORDERS 85

IV. THE PROPHETIC 97
   10. NEEDING A NEW "WORD" 97
   11. REDISCOVERING *DAMAH* 106
   12. THE DYNAMICS OF *DAMAH* 113
   13. MISCARRIED METAPHORS 128

V. THE PERIL 145
   14. FEELING OUR WAY 145
   15. DIGITAL DEMONS 161

VI. CONCLUSION 171
   16. THE ASSURANCE OF HOPE 171

ABOUT THE AUTHOR 185

ENDNOTES 186

FOREWORD

Recently I attended a Christian convention, on a beautiful mountain, in a timeless setting. Australian Christians have gathered on this hill for many decades to find food for their souls. The message, the mountain, and the manner of preaching have never changed, not in 50 years. Then I read this book by Thomas Hohstadt and I thought: not even a mountain top faith can survive the digital flood that is coming. Thomas Hohstadt has written a new book about the church. Not another book about the church . . . there are millions of them . . . but a new book. That is to say, it is a new book about the new church which is still somewhere over the digital horizon. I found the book both disturbing and exhilarating. It is disturbing because it rightly demonstrates that the church of yesterday and today is doomed. No amount of pentecostal fire is going to prevent the institutional church from burning to the ground. Indeed it is probably hastening the day. The book is exhilarating because Thomas has immense theological talent and learning. This book is not a doomsayers diatribe, but a prophet's vision wedded to a scholar's learning. This is a book about the digital revolution and its impact on the way in which we encounter the Word, and the way we form communities. The book also offers a powerful analysis of "this generation," which is the generation that is to inherit the digital earth. The 21st century church that they will inherit (and probably construct) is one that you and I can scarcely imagine. Our roots go back 500 years, and it is hard to think in any other terms than the church as we know it. The church of the 21st century has not even been planted yet, but Thomas has given us a clearer idea of what it is probably going to be like. This book is now on my table as a must book to share around.

Australia, 1999   **David Bell, Author, *Cyberchurch***

I. INTRODUCTION

1. APOCALYPTIC VISIONS

Something big is happening. And it will forever change the Church.

Historians call it the greatest watershed ever recorded. "If the world has not come to its end," Solzhenitsyn writes, "it has approached a major turn in history." Because—Alvin Toffler explains—"We are the final generation of an old civilization and the first generation of a new one."

Time magazine applied the same apocalypse:

> The 1990s have become a transforming boundary between one age and another, between a scheme of things that is disintegrating and another that is taking shape. A millennium is coming, a cosmic divide. The 20th century is an almost extinct volcano; the 21st is an embryo.[1]

Without doubt, something old has been dying, and something new is being born.

"A Means to Revelation"

We call this death "postmodernism." "Postmodernism" points to the end of the modern world . . . the collapse of current civilization . . . the crumbling of old laws . . . the tearing of social fabric. . . .

. . . or, simply the "death of culture."

At the same time, the way we think is crossing new thresholds. Already, our cold logic—our "absolute" truth—is surrendering to something new. We are seeing with different eyes and hearing with different ears. Even reality itself is changing! It's not that two and two are no longer four, it's just that two and two are no longer the issue.

This new reality means we are also speaking a new language—not just new words, but a new way of using words. Implicit words are replacing explicit words. Metaphoric words are replacing literal words. Endless flowing images are replacing orderly ideas. Experience is replacing reason. And feeling is replacing form.

In all these, "hidden" meanings are replacing rigorous definitions. Yet, these hidden meanings—Scripture proved ages ago—serve "as a means to revelation."[2]

From Dogma to Depth

The church—as a human institution—clings to the same dying culture. So the same death and the same rebirth haunt believers as well.

Church scholars, for example, call this the "end of the Reformation." Loren B. Mead claims, "God is dismantling the denominational systems as fast as possible."[3] And Robert Webber insists we already live in a "post-Christian" culture.

We find this first in reports of church attendance. Mainline churches have seen a slow, painful collapse since their peak in 1963. The Catholic Church has experienced a crisis in priestly callings, and many disenchanted Protestants who returned to the market-driven mega-churches are leaving again.

As a result, Christianity has lost its privileged position in the world. In truth, it has become a "subculture."[4] Just look around! In urbane, urban centers like New York City, more spiritually sensitive seekers go to the Metropolitan Museum of Art on Sundays than to cathedrals.[5]

Yet, not all is lost. In place of "religion," we are seeing a "post-religious spirituality"[6] We are tracking a new trail from the mind to the heart . . . from rhetoric to revelation . . . from public to private . . . from institution to individual . . . from external to internal.

In short, from dogma to depth.

A Thief in the Night

This trail leads not only to the birth of a new spirituality, but the birth of a new culture as well. And this new culture manifests mostly on the Internet—a metaphor of the future.

The Internet is the fastest growing medium the world has known. "There has never been any technology or innovation in human history that comes close in speed of adoption, significance, and impact."[7] "The number of Internet users is expected to nearly quadruple over the next five years at an average annual rate of 79 percent."[8]

It will power the future. Without doubt, "the digital revolution will set the course of the world."[9] Its massive and pervasive global network will, indeed, create a new planetary culture.

It's called the "information superhighway," and it can do amazing things. Fiber optics the size of a human hair, for example, can deliver every issue ever made of the *Wall Street Journal* in less than one second. And—like a thief in the night—the cunning power of this digital demon has broken into every area of modern living.

Even the Pope confesses, "The computer has changed my life."[10]

That's because this new media is changing the way we think. In the digital frontier, for example, the rules for survival and success are changing. And, like a force of nature, the change is irrevocable . . . unstoppable.

There's no turning back.

Make no mistake. What we see today, is not the digital age—it will reach critical mass just around the corner. The change we've known in the past is not the change we'll know in the future—the New Millennium will render life as we know it obsolete while something new struggles for survival. And the science of today is not the science of tomorrow—cyberspace will be a "virtual" reality . . . a "metaphorical" space.

What does this menacing change mean for the Church? It means we have entered a high-stakes battle in an amoral, post-modern world. It means we are in a race for the entire planet's faith—both "on-line" and "off-line."

> "Behold, I am doing a new thing!
> Now it springs forth; do you not
> perceive and know it and will you
> not give heed to it?"[11]

Moneyed Myopia

These predictions will occur sooner than we think. We're not waiting for some invention. It's already here, and things are taking place earlier than even extremists had believed.

Earlier upheavals moved with slow, blood-drenched dramas of war, revolt, famine, and other calamities. Even positive events resulted from the forward march of expected progress. And, though the experience of time has speeded up, we have never lost the feeling of continuity.

But tomorrow will be different. It won't continue the same faster pace, it will shift suddenly. It won't reveal itself one step at a time, it will appear instantly. It won't improve the past, it will break with the past. Like living inside a kaleidoscope, the New Millennium will shock us with amazing metamorphosis . . . exponential change . . . and crystalizing revolution.

For the first time, the future will unfold with "warp velocity." And with the old culture quickly crumbling, there is nothing firm on which to stand; so the shaking hands of even the experts paint small, blurred pictures. All the while, someone larger than us is painting a giant fresco, but we're so close to it we can't see it!

The church can't move into the future with past paradigms. The world is full of well-intentioned, church growth experts who peddle formulas, programs, and techniques. But old paradigms . . . old management styles . . . or any warmed-over idea masquerading as something new can't grasp the change that is engulfing us on a global scale.

Worldly economists, for example, report that innovation profits drive most digital data, but their moneyed myopia also misses the real picture. Other shortsighted observers misread the "information" in the "information age." Cyberspace, after all, means much more than information.

Guardians of Grace

How should the church respond?

The great historian Arnold Toynbee said we face crises in one of four ways: (1) We retreat—like turtles, (2) we trust—like lambs led to slaughter, (3) we tremble—like paranoids looking for demons, or (4) we take hold of the crisis and transform it into something useful.

Many of us in the church face crises the first way—we retreat into the past. The past remains our savior, so—as good guardians of grace—we turn our clocks back to a "golden age" . . . we lock ourselves into another time and place. Indeed, some of us spend all of our resources on old causes.

Sadly, we forget "human hands had been at work through the centuries"—in honor of our small memories—"probing and fumbling, and not always very happily."[12] We don't realize our churches have often become halls of mirrors where we see only our own reflections. We fail to grasp that our reputed "truth" feels good simply because it is in harmony with our own biases and bigotries.

Of course . . . the past can also be right.

But often, old and impotent models have lost their ability to empower the future. Often, past seasons of revelation have become dead metaphors in a new era. And often, our love for the "familiar" only tells of a time and place where God once was.

As a result, we mistake the oyster for the pearl. We confuse culture for content. We misread metaphor for message.

The symbols of faith replace faith itself.

> "O Jerusalem, Jerusalem . . . How often I have desired and yearned to gather your children together [around Me], as a hen [gathers] her young under her wings, but you would not!"[13]

Passive Ploys

Second, we blindly trust. Our confident assurance shows more flesh than faith. We simply ignore the threatening realities of the coming world. We simply hold to the status quo and try to do what we've been doing a little better.

In the meantime, we "just say no" to computers.

Or, we ward off the digital demons with another "quick fix." We assent to "an entertainment fix, a self-esteem fix, a self righteousness fix, or a self-help fix."[14] But the church remains the same. We are no more prepared for the future than before.

It's as if we were placing temporary bandages over mortal wounds.

Even improving the present won't work. What the church has today won't work tomorrow. The problems of today cannot be solved by the same mind-sets that created these problems in the first place. For tomorrow will render irrelevant all of our passive ploys.

After all, admission to the twenty-first century will cost us something. There is a price to pay.

> "There are three things which come
> not back—the spent arrow, the spo-
> ken word, and the lost opportunity."

Traditional

Specious Scapegoats

Third, we tremble. We avoid truth by looking for external enemies. We blame all of our problems on "the evil forces of the age." We become the pious paranoid . . . the "religious" spirits . . . and the fearful fanatics "with twitching nostrils who can sniff out heresy at a hundred kilometers."[15]

Consider Saint Augustine who said Christians should avoid those who can add or subtract, because they had obviously "made a covenant with the Devil."[16]

In this strategy there's a strange tragedy. Our rebellious youth and advanced technologies are not the enemies of the Church. At this moment, in fact, they are our only hope. If we fail the future, the blame will fall, instead, on our fleshly pride . . .

. . . disguised as "religion."

So we need to reflect Toynbee's fourth reaction: We need to take hold of the crisis and transform it into something useful. The other three problem solvers try to make things go away, but here, we try to bring new things into being.

When new paradigms appear, mere appearances had better disappear.

No Longer New

Some observers point to the success of the fastest growing churches as God's answer for the future. These churches have been called many things: charismatic, Pentecostal, free, independent, praise and worship. . . . And, no doubt, they came in with a roaring fire. Their Pentecostal origins early this century claimed "an 'end to history,' a 'new age,' and a 'postmodern era' long before any of these currently fashionable terms were invented."[17]

Sometimes called "post-denominational," they are neither Protestant nor Catholic. And—in the traditional sense—they are not even a "religion"! Yet, they remain the fastest growing churches in the world.

Some scholars believe they are the "new paradigm" church. And, true enough, they were new at one time. But no longer. These believers participate in their own passing paradigm.

For the "new paradigm church" does not yet exist!

The tragedy in this movement stems from the way it ties itself to the secular market. Its pristine power has too often turned crassly commercial. It asks a trendy, secular society what it wants the church to be, then it canonizes their craze as "eternal truth."

Yes, each age casts its own shadow. Yes, each generation follows the curvature of its own culture. These secular meditations are to be expected. But today, worship responds too often to trendsetters in a moneyed market . . . to apologists for the secular world . . . to propagandists in a worldly theocracy.

When these things happen, the world squeezes the church into its own fleshly mold . . . its own biased blindness . . . its own particular prejudice. Then we confuse the "spirit of our time" with the spirit of worship. Then we find religious "experience" a slippery notion.

For we can no longer tell gold from dross.

Jekyll and Hyde

So nothing in our past totally prepares us for the future. With deep affection, we hope that our older, more precious metaphors will still speak with power in the New Millennium. But God's creative power will astound us:

"We are at the front edges of the greatest transformation of the Church." "It may eventually make the transformation of the Reformation look like a ripple in a pond."[18] That's because the future promises a spiritual event, not just a technological discovery . . . it promises the wisdom of the heart, not just the intellect of the mind . . . it promises values and visions, not just bytes and bits.

With these promises, the Church can lead again! It can lead history rather than follow it. New life can birth from decaying old life. New order can emerge from distressing disorder.

Yet, without our leadership, the future will go the other way. For it is a Jekyll and Hyde future where the winner takes all.

Marshall McLuhan saw, but never precisely stated, that highly advanced electronic media in the hands of bankrupt spirits will soon destroy us. Because a medium that works with the speed of light requires a Spirit of Light. The power of the Internet works for good only if we are good. It surfs safely only if we savor certainty . . .

. . . that is, only if we live in the Truth.

Already the Internet races out of control. Cyberspace is a place of no laws . . . no restraints. It has turned into an impulsive monster—reckless, confused, uncertain, and dangerous. Even its inventors fear what it may become.[19]

If we don't get our act together—and soon!—the church could suffer a great tragedy in our refusal to see God's hand in this apocalyptic event. The twenty-first century already evokes images of spiritual wars and end-time disasters.

So we must prepare for action. We must leave behind all of our excess baggage. We must redefine ourselves for the digital age. We must set a revolutionary agenda. Yes, we always confess Christ "the same, yesterday, today . . . and forever"[20] But we must also expertly adapt His story to the demands of the digital age.

In this postmodern age, "Can we sing the Lord's song in a strange land?"

We must!

A Compass for the Future

This book prepares the church for a future of change. It confronts the hidden tyrannies among the most revered traditions and reveals the glorious promises among the most feared trends. It tells how we got here, where we're going, and secrets to a successful transition.

Perhaps most important, it gives a glimpse of God's nature in a new worldly order.

For that reason, this book is not the typical "church growth" book. It does not stand on past paradigms. It does not warm up yesterday's management techniques. It does not pitch old ideas as something new. Instead, it provides a compass that can guide us to a place where no one has ever been.

It paints an accurate picture of the driving forces in the emerging era and presents the astounding opportunities for the New Millennium Church. It describes a new Word for a new age . . . a divine Word for a digital age . . . a transcendent metaphor for a transcendent moment. It lovingly and honestly lays to rest the lost legacies of the past, and describes the "digital demons" of the future . . . or more important, how the church will defeat them.

In short, this book navigates the church through the stormy waters of our approaching time.

2. HOW WE GOT HERE . . .

Parallel Paths

Communication informs reality and the way we live. Indeed, the way we worship and the way we communicate trace precisely parallel paths. In the next two chapters, we follow these paths—starting with the first century oral tradition, turning next to the printing press, focusing then on television, and, finally, foreseeing the digital future.

In the absence of "the pure in heart," the way we communicate decides who we are, because *what* we see in the world comes from the *way* we see it. And the way we see it filters through the medium of the message.

The world creates media machines in its own image, then these machines—in turn—recreate the world in their image. Worldly souls love to stand transfixed in these mirrors of self-adoration. . . .

. . . until visionaries discover a new medium. Then—breathlessly — one civilization surrenders itself, and another smashes old narcissistic spells.

The church needs to stay awake and watch these forces at work. It must discern both the hidden blessings and the dark dominions . . . then move safely into the next paradigm.

We must know how we got here . . . why our traditions differ . . . why some churches grow . . . why others die . . . which trends will mainstream . . . and how we anticipate our changing roles.

Hammering Screws

Sorrowfully, churches usually lag several years behind. Most of the talk about "where the church is going" is really "where the church has been." Today's so-called "cutting-edge" is already past history. The success models of yesterday simply won't work tomorrow.

None of them describe the Church of the New Millennium.

And for good reason. Every communication medium focuses on its strengths while ignoring its weaknesses. It emphasizes what it does well while excluding what it does not do well. It highlights those things within its view while biasing everything beyond its view.

That's why we lock into the legacy of one medium and ignore the vision of a new one. We misread the signs of the times and react to the wrong issues. We blame the "forces of evil" and miss the actual historical realities.

In short, we attack new paradigms with old tools. Rex Miller[1] compares our stupidity to using a hammer on a screw. The wrong tool. The wrong results.

Things get destroyed.

These damaged remnants remain in today's churches. Like broken genetic codes, three distinct traditions cling to their lost legacies. And, now, a new medium once again severs the past from the future . . . and its victims from its victors.

We describe these media, their remnants and the amazing changes that lie ahead.

The Oral Tradition

Of all the "words"—of all the media—the oral tradition remains the most personal and powerful. But—though we still talk to one another—we know nothing of the oral tradition. This medium gave birth to Christianity and transformed the Western World. Yet, today, our Greek rhetoric words, our hollow dictionary definitions, and our shallow television images survive as trivial cousins to their ancient oral ancestors.

The Catholic Church emerged first from the oral tradition of the early Christians. Indeed, ritualized sounds, aromas, tastes, movements, architecture, and poetry—all elements of the oral tradition—defined its worship. But by then, Christianity had become the "political" religion of the worldly Roman Empire, and worship had become a "spectator" event for its citizens. So today, liturgical services only vaguely recall the oral tradition.

Our routine rituals remain only relics . . . only residues.

The oral tradition of the ancient Hebrews was—in the beginning—an "inspired" word . . . a prophetic word . . . a "word" within a word . . . in fact, *more* than a word. Unlike modern words—known only by the brain—Hebrew "words" emerged first from the body. For Hebrew flesh uttered felt meanings . . . metaphorical sensations . . . endless sensuous shades.

Their bodies talked!

These were visceral feelings that spoke more from the intuitive heart than the logical mind. Then the Hebrews boldly shared these feelings with others through story, song, image, dance, and portrayal.

In short, oral "words" were prophetic . . . prophecies were
metaphoric . . . and metaphors were artistic. All essential syn-
onyms! But their "art" was not the art of today. Oral "words," for
example, were as simple as Jesus "breaking bread" or "mixing clay
with spit."[2]

And, unlike today, these "words" were used with great
care—they were introduced with great intention. "Believing" and
"speaking," for example, were always the same. Like adoring
imitators of their Father, the early Hebrews spoke "of nonexistent
things . . . as if they [already] existed." They declared "the end and
the result from the beginning."[3]

It was the privilege of boldness.

It's no surprise that in the middle of a drought and under dry
skies, Elijah claimed, "There is the sound of abundance of rain."[4]
Nor was it unusual when Jesus declared, "I have overcome the
world," when—in reality—His victory became fact when He later
died and rose again.[5]

So most important, oral "words" had power—not the power
of the heroic ego, but a spiritual power greater than the speaker.
And the speaker fully expected something awesome to happen.
Each moment was charged with raw reality . . . immediate possibility . . . manifest presence.

Because God was a God of history who endlessly created
new things.

The Hebrews knew that the "Word" of God and the Spirit
of God were the same thing. And they knew from experience that
the "word" they spoke went forth and did things . . . moved with
creative power . . . fulfilled its own prophecy . . . manifested its own
meaning. Unlike today's words which merely "supervene" in

life—that is, they only "add to" life—oral words "intervened" in life—they actually "changed life."

Power incarnated power.

We find these oral "words" in the sounds of the trumpets that flattened the walls of Jericho. We find them in the music of David's lyre that drove an evil spirit from Saul. And we find them in the voices of the prophetic singers that led Judah's army while God defeated their foes.

Carl Hausman claims metaphors like these "are active forces in the world" . . . that they have the power to bring "something into being."[6] And Paul Ricoeur promises metaphors have "the power not only to generate meaning but ultimately to change the world."[7] In other words, prophetic metaphors can still empower the Church today!

The Print Medium

But something happened in the meantime. . . .

About 550 years ago, Gutenberg invented movable type. Though not earthshaking in itself, he catalyzed a revolution already underway.[8] Unaware, he took the trends of machine, logic, and individualism and exploded them into a new reality that reigned until just recently.

Indeed, we can credit the Reformation more to Gutenberg's Bible than to Luther's theses. And today's reformed churches[9] stand as direct descendants of this revolution.

Of course, the written word had existed long before Gutenberg's invention. But when print became the dominant medium, everyone stood in line to take advantage of it. Sequential alphabets created strings of words . . . strings of words created sequences of thoughts . . . sequences of thoughts created logic . . . and logic created society.

Almost that simple.

With the printed page, ideas could be locked in space and time. Then, they could be rearranged, added to, compared, contrasted, critiqued . . . breeding books about books about books.
. . .

The church changed.

Truth traced to rational scholarship—ideas based on ideas . . . doctrines built on doctrines. The sermon took center stage with commentaries *about* the Bible replacing the Bible itself. The "Word" became concepts about concepts. . . . And faith became an intellectual conclusion . . . an accepted idea . . . a "reason" for life.

Yes, we found benefits. The written word knows its strength. Objectivity birthed a new science and a new scholarship. Recorded history improved our honesty and our memory. Reading skills brought authority to the individual and priesthood to the believer.

Also, we found that written languages and laws traveled well, allowing new empires and widely dispersed armies. Indeed, "the pen proved mightier than the sword."

But, finally, we found problems in the "fine print" of the printed medium. The rights of the individual turned to rampant individualism. And an omniscient, omnipresent, omnipotent God was often reduced to a mere idea . . . a distant concept. Indeed, God was whoever writers and readers decided He was.

Though the heroic, literal mind did not totally destroy our senses and symbols, it did subordinate them. Or—more truthfully—our feelings were dis-incarnated and then stamped on dead trees.

The Word was no longer "flesh."

As the print medium became more static, linear, rigid, and academic, boards became bureaucratic . . . laws became legalism . . . pieties became protocols . . . and high honors became hierarchy.

It was law without life.

The powers of print continued in the Western World until the 1960's. Then their dominance ended. Today, their dying breaths whisper an old paradigm, and their "reformed" churches wheeze the same old song.[10]

The Electronic Medium

Even before the twilight of empowered print, the electronic age tuned in with radio and then transfigured the scene with television. By the 1950's, television had already planted the seeds that would finally choke out the print tradition.

It was the "age of broadcast."

The powerful elite pushed a new "word"—in moving images—at passive masses. Communication became an aggressive one-way street—from the one to the many . . . from the powerful to the powerless . . . from the literate to the increasingly illiterate.

Soon, the far-reaching language of television became our "first language" . . . the dominant mode of thought . . . the seamless part of our lives. And a new visual "word" slammed the door on old-fashioned printed logic and its obedient cousin, spoken rhetoric. One visionary pastor, admits, "The sermon as we have known it is dead."[11]

For we now live in what Doris Lessing calls a "sensate culture"—an environment of senses and feelings. Excitement validates events, events validate experience, and experience validates truth. The "Word," in other words, "happens"! It penetrates, pushes, and imprints our passions.

So in this revolution, we privilege the subjective over the cerebral . . . the revealed over the reasonable . . . and the internal over the external. And in this new reality, we prefer spirituality to religion . . . desirability to doctrines . . . and sensuality to certitude.

Because "certitude" has been replaced by flowing images. Orderly ideas have been dethroned by speeding realities. It is a continuous, discontinuous world.

Jazz-like . . . collage-like.

For these reasons, reality has become temporal, changeable, ephemeral. Fleeting televised images have washed out the past and created endless cravings for the "latest and greatest." No wonder our children wander aimlessly with shorter and shorter attention spans. No wonder their channel flicking has become such a trivial art.

But television, alone, was not enough. . . .

A Second Reformation

Like the printing press, television catalyzed revolutions already underway. It empowered trends already emerging. In the realm of the spirit, for example, it tapped into raging underground seas of raw religious feelings and gave them shape and expression.

These passionate undercurrents—always counter-cultural, always outside mainstream religion—began decades ago as a quickening series of "holy spirit revivals" that continue, even now, to engulf each other.[12]

But spirit-filled old-timers didn't make the difference. It was the dispossessed youth of the '60's—the first generation raised on television—that made the difference. After "tuning in, turning on, and dropping out," many of these rebels became the "Jesus freaks" or hippie-Christians whose spiritual ecstasies echoed with the youth of the world. Music was their language, and their simple choruses birthed the "praise and worship" movement that later swept through virtually every form of Christianity.

In other words, three mighty streams created the new church of the '90's: the spontaneous power of holy spirit revivals, the rebellious tangents of the '60's children, and the surface sensuality of the television medium.

What can we call this church? In truth, it defies all previous descriptions. It not only refuses the "Protestant" label, but it even resists what we would normally call "religion"! It has been labeled "post-denominational," "charismatic," "Pentecostal," "independent," "nondenominational," and "free." But all these terms grow more outdated, and in the third world—where this church expands the fastest—such labels have no meaning at all.

One thing for certain, this movement proves powerful. Harvard's Harvey Cox calls it "deeply liberating and empowering" and "the most important event in religious history since the Reformation."[13] "It is hardly a debatable question," echoes Fuller's Peter Wagner, that this new church "has now taken its place on the cutting edge of the worldwide extension of the Kingdom of God."[14]

The Sacred Within the Profane

So what is this church like?

First, it is more individual than institutional . . . more independent than dependent . . . more personal than professional. Its members are "more like tourists exploring the religious terrain in search of fragments of truth and insight."[15] That's the reason you can't find this church in the year book of the American and Canadian Churches or the directory of the World Council of Churches.

Second, it speaks the language of pop culture. Indeed, the shifting sand of secular sanctity provides the anchor for this fractious movement. The twentieth century had already faced toward popular culture, but this church made it an about-face:

It looks for the sacred *within* the profane.[16]

Finally, this church is market driven . . . "customer sensitive." Whatever "attracts and holds a crowd is seen as that which God endorses."[17] As a result, its market place leaders strive toward a success-equals-numbers dream with endless "packaged" products of slick entertainment.

More to the point, this church is theatrical. Its leaders design their sanctuaries as theaters. They "perform" the Word . . .

that is, they "turn it on" with "turned on" lights, sound, music and preaching. Of course, superstars carry the day, while their glory "groupies" listen passively and vicariously to their spiritual idols.

"The Best of Times/ The Worst of Times"

The movement has both wonderful traits and woeful woes.

To begin, "new wine skins" do promise refreshment. But new packaging alone only brings an addiction to the "new and improved." Still, freedom from an irrelevant past does bring relief. But how often do we "throw the baby out with the bath water"? Nevertheless, the Church must always be counter-cultural. But when we embrace a secular culture, how can we—at the same time—be counter-cultural?

Certainly, we must reach the unchurched through a popular language. But popular spirituality—by definition—must come with simple and easy pleasure. So, too often, our spirituality manifests a cosmetic, neutered, Muzak version of the real thing. We end up not only "in the world," but "of the world." Then . . . instead of the "Word becoming flesh," the "flesh becomes the Word."

Have we forgotten Paul's witness? "We don't take God's Word, water it down, and then take it to the streets to sell it cheap."[18]

Nonetheless, we must relate the Gospel to the reality of life . . . to immediate needs. But a market-driven medium that only creates consumer "itches" will bring relevance without depth . . . selfishness without selflessness . . . blessings without blessing.

Granted, there is nothing wrong with inspired, relevant speakers. Unless, of course, our worship focuses on them as star-performers, and they draw us into their personality cults while we watch passively from our pews like TV "couch potatoes." Have we forgotten the lessons of both Scripture and history? Have we, once again, asked someone else to be our mediator with God?

Have we, once again, lost our own priesthood?

Even when forceful speakers "provoke us to good works," is our joy half-hopeful and half-"hypeful"? When a big personality pumps us up, can we tell the difference between natural, spiritual, and even demonic emotions? After all, if we carelessly "turn on" emotions that have no definitions . . . no guidelines . . . and no cautions, we can claim anything in the name of our feelings.

If a movement bases its theology on emotion, it had better know the difference between natural, spiritual, and demonic emotions.

Finally, we must agree that the spontaneity, freedom, and openness of this church are surely Christian principles. And liberation from man-made doctrines is certainly welcome. But embracing the world's "relative" truth is no better . . . and going with the world's "relaxed" morals no improvement. Where the print medium proclaimed "law without life," too many of us now proclaim "life without law."

Will this new church last?

Yes . . . if it changes.

3. . . . WHERE WE'RE GOING

The Digital Future

Once again, a new medium moves a new mood . . . a new promise pushes a new paradigm . . . a new style sows a new seed. The results will prove unavoidable, and they "will be very different from the electronic church that we know from television."[1]

Futurists usually combine radio, television, and computer technology into one "electronic" medium. Rex Miller, however, clearly sees a major difference between the "electronic" age and our "digital" future. His vision inspired this chapter.

The first computer network appeared about 1969. Then, the '80's saw digital technology as the driving force of the future. By 1994, the World Wide Web had taken a firm foothold. And today, this new technology even drives the world's stock markets.

In other words, the ground has shifted before a full generation has grown up with this new model.

Church leaders have largely missed this change because they see only hype for what appears to be glorified office machines. True, the information highway may be mostly hype today, but it is an understatement about tomorrow. It may seem a vague matter of the future, but it will totally change the church.

Future historians will probably pick the year 2,000 as the watershed moment. Whatever the year, the Internet already stands as a metaphor of what will soon amplify human will and purpose at a staggering rate . . . and at a global level.

What will this new church look like?

We already know.

Natural Enemies

Mirroring the births of the print and electronic media, computers also empower trends already underway. And—like the '60's youth in their time—the 90's youth embody these trends. But today's "boomers" have forgotten society's refusal of the youthful Jesus Movement in the '60's and 70's, so—once again—church leaders are misreading the trends and risking the loss of today's young.

We forget that the instincts and desires of the '60's youth have become mainstream in our churches today. We seem unaware that the radical ideas of the rebellious baby boomers are now routine. So we continue forcing our postmodernism on the '90's youth just when postmodernism may be disappearing.[2] And we flaunt our hippie-ish "New Age" beliefs just when we're entering a post-hippie age.[3]

The '90's youth are not baby boomers. In fact, today's youth and our boomer church leaders are natural enemies! The subculture of the young deplores boomer values. It despises the soulish narcissism of its New Age elders. It detests the hollowness of their commercial spirituality. And, as a result, it screams visceral hostility to any boomer institution that tells it what to believe.

For their part, the boomers scorn the young's irreverent and vulgar videos and movies. They turn in disgust from their aggressively unpretty grunge clothes, pierced noses, and tatoos. And they can't stand the in-your-face sassiness and arrogance of its no-commitment "slackers."

This mutual animosity is more than a generation gap. It's a paradigm shift . . . a total misunderstanding. The boomers have failed to see the unseen sorrows of the first generation of "latch-key" kids . . . the despairs of their commonly broken homes . . . or the absurdities of television as surrogate parents.

The boomers have forgotten that these kids are the first to really sense the absence of moral absolutes . . . the first children to be robbed of their character . . . and, undoubtedly, the last generation to trust in institutional religion.

The boomers overlook the fact that these kids grew up in a time of economic setback . . . that they are both unemployed and underemployed . . . and that there is no way they can pay for the boomers' old-age social security.

No wonder the young are angry, broken, lonely, and rootless. No wonder they show a world-weariness beyond their years. No wonder they struggle so much with the boomers' version of success.

But . . . the '90s youth know something! They know a future for which the boomers haven't a clue. They have earned a spirituality—though far-out and foreign—that reaches to a greater depth than that of their elders. And they move easily and knowingly in the language and learning of the digital age.

The boomers will someday ask their forgiveness.

The Lord's Song in a Strange Land

If the Church is to sing its song in the New Millennium, we must first hear the echoing themes between youthful trends and digital technology. For the same sounds that now resonate through the '90's youth movement and the digital age also resounded in the First Millennium Church: a new knowledge . . . a new creativity . . . a new community . . . a new freedom . . . and a new empowerment.

Like the ancient Hebrews, today's youth measure knowledge by experience. Their bodies often know things before their minds do . . . they are more spiritual than cognitive.

In short, they see no distinction between spirit and body . . . mind and emotion.

In place of mandated facts, for example, they prefer raw experience. Rather than traditional doctrines, they desire altered states. Instead of left-sided brains, they crave multisensory worlds.

Nonetheless, they're still looking for God . . . but not in the traditional places! In fact, they find their most meaningful spiritual experiences in popular culture. The prophetic metaphors . . . chance imageries . . . implicit visions . . . and endless communions in their movies, videos, CD's, and Internet dialogue give them a church-like experience—emotional, uplifting . . . even caring.

(In fact, their world proves vastly more spiritual than the earlier pop culture of the boomers.)

Some currents within today's secular stream "are sufficient to begin funding a new theology by, for, and about a generation."[4] And the fact that many of their images are irreverent and angry mean more a longing for faith than a rejection of faith.

In all these new images, today's youth have seen something everyone else has missed: They intuitively know that the "language" of language has forever changed. They don't care anymore for religious codes and clichés. They refuse the boomer's force-fed "five steps to spiritual victory." For they consider sequential thought outdated and logical words a form of manipulation.

Most postmodern scholars agree.

Market driven churches have replaced this problem with a show-business spirituality, but these TV-savvy youngsters are sickened by such unseemly hype. And no longer can their elders sell the latest New Age line, for today's youth see an end to what they call "cocktail spirituality."

Clearly, a new way of sharing the Word is needed. Clearly, the church needs to reach the youth. It needs those who will carry the gospel into the New Millennium.

And, gratefully, the future can meet these needs: The digital age will soon present a multimedia, multisensory, virtual-realty world designed especially for today's youth and their new language—the language of prophetic metaphor.

The Church can learn to "sing the Lord's song in a strange land."[5]

A New Creativity and a New Community

The youth intuitively understand that God is the great Creator, not the great Imitator! And in this truth, we find another example of the harmonizing trends between kids and computers.

Today's youth turn from anything routine, boring, and predictable to anything imaginative, energizing, and innovative. They would rather create their own business, for example, than push pencils in a large corporation.

So, again, they are children of their time, for the digital age is an innovation-based economy. Inventive ideas and creative insights are its very products. Even the medium speaks the language of creativity. Virtual reality—mirroring faith itself—endlessly "calls those things that be not as though they were."

In the same way, their community also reflects the coming digital community; for popular culture is their community, and their peers their congregation. They have, as example, refused the passive, spectator worship of the boomers and the illusory community of television "couch potatoes." Instead, they demand participation . . . dialogue . . . interaction. . . .

And this, too, signals the coming age, for their new "community is the new commodity."[6] We have left the one-to-many broadcast medium and are entering a one-to-one digital medium. "Interaction," "interdependency," "collaboration," and "dialogue" are the new buzzwords. Common interests now draw the young together into common communities.

There is something spiritual about this. The idea of connecting to one another in another space is inherently spiritual. The notion of a "covenant network" of allied individuals is certainly Christian. And—for the first time—the promised "body of Christ" is potentially global.

A New Freedom and a New Empowerment

Freedom is another shared theme. The youth are bound to break the barriers of time, space, geography, gender, and generation. Given a chance, they will do their "thing," and the Internet will give them that chance. They feel at ease in an ethnically diverse world, and—behind a computer screen—think whatever they want to think and become whoever they want to become.

Their music, for example, draws its energy from breaking the barriers of both time and space. They easily celebrate past popular styles and sincerely welcome a variety of global traditions.

In a similar way, the Internet will enter the same excluded paths . . . invade the same restricted areas . . . and cross the same forbidden borders. It will reach anyone, anywhere, anytime, anyway. Or—modeling the new Church—it will reach "different" souls in "different" places at "different" times and in "different" ways.

And, finally, we can compare computers and kids in the new power shift. It may come as a surprise to boomers, but the young are now in charge! This is the first generation brought up with computers, and it forms a global network of young entrepreneurs that know how to start businesses fast and run them cheap. In truth, a twenty-year-old, who feels at home with this new technology, has more potential to change the world than many corporations.

They will be the leaders of the new cyberculture . . . the gurus of the ascending geek culture.

In the digital age, anyone can become an initiator of innovation and change. Fluency in the new medium is now more powerful than size and number. Indeed, a grain of sand (silicon) is worth more than an ounce of gold when innovation is etched on its surface.

In this paradigm shift, the huge institutions of the boomers will become unwieldy burdens. But the young will have the world in their digital hands!

Entering a New "Holy of Holies"

If the church can open the hearts of today's youth, it can open the doors to the New Millennium. But this "openness" must be on their terms. And their terms require the church of the future to enter a new "holy of holies."

To reach these youth, we must first feel their deep pain. We must know their tortured and alienated souls as the driving force of their lives. After all, they knew suffering as a spiritual experience long before the boomers even considered the idea. And, finally, we must agree they are, indeed, searching for God . . . but in a totally new way and with a totally new language.

Their search for community, though, represents their most desperate need. In truth, they never recovered from their broken homes. They long for a sense of belonging, and the church would do well in responding to their needs.

But responding to their needs doesn't mean one more church program. They are skeptical of "programs" . . . of anything "organized." True, they welcome honesty and authenticity—in any form—but they have learned to be suspicious of institutions and authority figures.

They have already tasted too much pretension and pretending. After all, Christianity is not a program . . . not a board of directors . . . not a hierarchy . . . not a denomination . . . not a building . . . not a governing structure. These truths should make us pause.

The youth want the church to *be* the Church—not to be something it isn't or to be a counterfeit version of what it pretends to be. They want a community built around loving relationships rather than hairsplitting doctrines. They want a community sensitive to their multiple stages of growth, learning, and ministry rather than anonymity in the boomers' favorite programs.

They want a flexible community with alliances crossing all denominations, traditions, and cultures. They want worship, fun, and teaching *anyplace* (though perhaps not in the church building!) and *anytime* (though perhaps not on Sunday morning!).

Transcendent Messages

If the boomers differ this much from today's youth, how will they communicate?

First, boomers must be real. They must really believe what they say, and what they say must be relevant to youthful lives. In the same way, boomers must relate to the youth—without condescension or manipulation—as individuals, rather than as "Generation X," "Baby Busters," or anything else. For the youth seek "user-friendly" acceptance, without guilt, shame, or pigeonholes.

In short, they want a *two-way* relationship. They want to participate . . . interact.

Next, boomers must learn to speak the language of the youth—the language of cutting-edge, popular culture. But, within that language, boomers must convey transcendent images, words, and actions that carry an *implicit*—rather than explicit—message. In other words, youth want room to be equally inspired to draw their own conclusions.

These "implicit" messages promise a return of art to the Church. They pledge a reappearance of the poet/prophet. They perceive a rediscovery of the prophetic metaphor. And the youth will listen to these messages. They will listen to inspiration, spontaneity, and transcendence . . . the off-the-wall . . . the relentlessly fresh and new.

For they think in flowing nanosecond images. They feel at home in multisensory, multimedia environments. In fact, they can take in more information in less time and with less confusion than their boomer elders. That's because they have learned to experience truth . . . rather than talk about it.

A Spirit of Adventure

Worship, then, must reflect the same respect . . . relevance . . . room . . . and rapport. This means an honest service controlled by the Holy Spirit rather than some authority figure . . . a service with more humility than hype . . . a service with more intimacy to God than subjection to an institution.

It means a safe, loving environment without threat or shame. It means a "family" setting without cold-shoulders from the boomers. It means plenty of room for reflective growth without pressure or manipulation.

Their worship is audience-prompted worship—collaborative, interactive. It carries a personal touch . . . an involvement in the outcome. Anything else is welcome as long as it is short, excellent, and doesn't interrupt the flow of participative worship.

Throughout, they want a sense of expectancy. They want worship that moves almost randomly . . . spontaneously. And variety is their theme: multisensory, multimedia, multidimensional, multicultural. . . .

In summary, they want their language, their style, their environment . . . but with an awesome twist!

It's the spirit of adventure.

A Continuing Relevance

Does the church see the signs of our time? The youth are protesting all the religious language that has turned stagnant. They are rejecting the mistaken idea that "God never does anything new." And they are refusing any religion thrust upon them without choice.

Make no mistake about it. They are going to do *something*, and they will have the power to do it. In ten years, half the world will be teens, and they will have more in common with their global peers than they will their boomer elders. The real division will not be between the have's and have not's, but between the young and everybody else!

The youth of the '90s already speak a digital language. It is their language. They will soon be producing full-motion, video term papers on their laptops. So we must take for granted they will be the innovators . . . the pioneers of the digital age.

In addition to their computer skills, they have special gifts for the new century. They are more informed than the previous generation and are not afraid of diversity or change. They are also proving tough and resilient, and—in the midst of their suffering—will already be older and wiser before they even start.

Is the church ready for them? This is no mere trend. There's a difference, after all, between "trends" and "transformations." Trends simply disengage the moment, but transformations shatter clichés and shock easy realities with new revelations.

No church leader wants to endure the trauma of change, but there are times when God alters the course of history. And, when that happens, everyone is expected to drop their excess baggage—their cherished traditions . . . their worn-out language . . . their privilege and power. For what made ministry effective in the past becomes a liability in the future.

No one is without feet of clay. It is not enough for past traditions to catch up with passing trends. The church must change or die.

And even with change, there remains a challenge, for the digital age promises just as much tragedy as triumph. Yet, if a New Millennium theology can be grounded in Christian principles, this promises our long-awaited victory.

II. THE PROMISE

4. "EXCEEDINGLY GREAT PROMISES"

Empowering to Empower

"We face the deepest creative restructuring of all time."[1] These words of Alvin Toffler echo, as well, the thoughts of Harvard's Harvey Cox: "We find evidence for a new phase of history in virtually every field of human endeavor."[2]

Including the church.

Church growth specialist Charles Arn sees a new paradigm which will rediscover life . . . a new lens which will reinterpret the world.[3] New Age scholar Rex Miller sees a new medium which will redefine society and change the way we worship.[4] And Canadian theologian David Lochhead sees a new awareness which will revise reality.[5]

"Mega-trend" . . . "metamorphosis" . . . "dramatic change" . . . "cataclysmic power" . . . historians are running out of superlatives. But they all agree this change—like a force of nature—stands irreversible . . . unstoppable!

They also agree we've entered a time where we will see life less rationally and more intuitively . . . less analytically and more holistically . . . less literally and more metaphorically. In short, we've shifted from an intellectual religion to personal spirituality

... from a God of philosophy to a God of prophecy ... from a God of apologetics to a God of apocalypse.

Indeed, historian William Irwin Thompson calls our time "a spiritual evolution." He says this "spiritual evolution" is actually creating the new technologies of a digital age ... it is midwifing the birth of a new humanity.[6] In other words, technology is not birthing a new spirit; Spirit is birthing a new technology!

Wake up church!

Increasingly, something is blowing open awe-inspired visions in fields like physics, biology, and astronomy. Increasingly, artists are witnessing a future far different from the materialism of the industrial age. Increasingly, spiritual awareness is reaching critical mass in the mystery of the New Millennium.

In short, the Lord of history is empowering a new Church.

Paving Cow Paths

But most can't see it. A "computer ministry," for example, doesn't make sense to the cynical: "There can no more be a theology of computers than there can be a theology of electric can openers."[7] "In short, 'cyberspace' is a silly fad!" And, in a way, these skeptics are right. As admitted earlier, "The information superhighway may be mostly hype today, but"—insists Nicholas Negroponte—"it is an *understatement* about tomorrow. It will exist beyond people's wildest predictions."[8]

Still, "How can 'bytes' and 'bits' be more valuable than bananas?" "We live in a material world, after all. We require food, clothing, shelter and all the other things of life. Certainly, material needs form the very backbone of our economy." And this is also true . . . if we look to the past. But wake up! Last night, "immaterial" things became the *new* economy.

Why are we so blind? Why can't we see where all this is taking us?

Because we confuse the present, so-called "digital age" with the *real* one just around the corner. To some of us, computers are just business tools—glorified typewriters, virtual filing cabinets, faster adding machines. At most, pious pacesetters find fleeting interest in Bibles on disks, word-processed sermons, e-mail, or traditional networking. But usually, we only automate old ways of working. Like paving cow paths, we simply place one technology on top of another.

Finally, some of us simply hate the computer. Rather than "user-friendly," we know this digital invader as "user-vicious." Indeed, we consider it a vile embodiment of all those things the Church rejects: the scheming mind without the heart . . . the automated world without freedom. And—like the tower of Babel—we believe God will surely punish all those cyber-punks who presume to be gods!

Projecting the Present

But the morality of computers is not even an issue. The hard fact is they're here. And no longer are computers about computing. They are about living! They will make the church different, and they will make the world different.

. . . at a fast pace. Negroponte noticed the Internet growing by 10 percent a month. He said at this rate, the total number of Internet users could exceed (if it were possible) the world population by 2003.[9] In secular terms, the Internet will become "the center of the universe," predicts Dennis Jones, CIO of Federal Express.

What will this new universe look like? How will the church change? We can tell by projecting our present experience. In the midst of chaotic change, predictive threads are appearing . . . implied patterns are emerging. God's Truth never changes, but the new church will reflect what we see and hear in the trends of current culture.

Hot-button words, for example, scream "innovation," "speed," and "power."

The computer, in other words, is first a creation of endless innovation . . . pure potentiality . . . boundless perspectives . . . in short, a "possibility machine"—limited only by our imagination. It will do virtually anything we want it to do. It will be almost anything we want it to be. And it will do it at the speed of light.

But most often, we hear the word, "powerful." For the computer represents the ultimate technology that completes and fulfills all other technologies. Lochhead writes,

> Our century has seen the development of at least three "ultimate technologies": nuclear technology, genetic engineering and computers . . . the power of cosmic destruction . . . the capacity to remake life . . . (and) an extension of the brain . . . machines that allow us to "play God."[10]

Informing the World

"Playing God," of course, brings grave dangers. Yet, Paul said, "Be *imitators* of God [copy Him and follow His example], as well-beloved children." And Peter agreed, "He has bestowed on us His precious and exceedingly great promises, so that . . . (we) become sharers (partakers) of the divine nature."[11]

Never before has the Church been given such a chance to fulfill its divine nature. For this Spirit-birthed age births spirit! The very dynamics that define the digital age will also define the Church: a new knowledge . . . a new creativity . . . a new community . . . a new freedom . . . and a new empowerment. To say the church has nothing to do with these dynamics—and the tools that make them possible—is to deny the Church itself!

Let's look at these trends and how they will empower the Church:

First, digital information is more than data. It "includes not simply logical and seemingly unemotional (facts), but values, the products of passion and emotion, not to mention imagination and intuition."[12] In its value-added form, in other words, information becomes knowledge, and knowledge becomes wisdom.

The computer now converges three industries: computing, communications, and content. But the biggest profits explode from content . . . intellectual property . . . meaningful knowledge.[13] "The fact that *TV Guide* has been known to make larger profits than all four networks combined suggests that the value of *information about information* (knowledge) can be greater than the value of the information itself."[14] More than ever, knowledge is the central resource of the world economy. More than ever, knowledge is power. More than ever, brains—not brawn—create value.

But the Church has always been an "information provider." For most of history, knowledge has been whatever the Church held it to be. Now—in the "information age"—the Church must continue communicating the "Good News" . . . but on a much grander scale!

Created to Create

Second, the new economy is an innovation-based economy . . . a creative-centered paradigm. So "human imagination becomes the main source of value."[15] Today, in fact, "The only sustainable competitive advantage is . . . innovation."[16] Why? Because ferocious competing forces drive a dazzling, ever-changing array of inventive ideas and creative insights.

But creativity also forms the foundation of faith. Our God is a Creator-God, so His New Creation is both now and not yet. Through inspired prophecy, God proclaimed to Isaiah, "Behold, I am doing a *new* thing . . . the former things have come to pass, and new things I now declare." In truth, God's very name speaks of creativity. In answer to Moses, He called Himself: "I-WILL-BE-WHAT-I-WILL-BE."

More to the point, our Creator-God created us in His image. That's the reason creativity pervades the entire Bible. The Bible's "religious language does not describe what is," according to Harvey Cox. Instead, "It describes what is coming to be." And this "coming to be" defines the creative process. It is implicit, for example, in the very meanings of faith, meditation, and prophecy.

Faith, after all, anticipates the yet-to-be. It looks "to things that are unseen" and "perceives" the things we hope for. Then it gives "substance" to its vision.[17] For if faith lacks deeds and actions to back it up--the disciple James declared--it has no power. Centering on the same creativity, meditation creates its contemplative visions in a dialogue with God. And prophecy does the same . . . but shares its visions with others.

So it follows that both Isaiah and the psalmist command, "Sing to the Lord a *new* song." For a true Christian work, says Dorothy Sayers "is the creation of something new."

In short, we were created to create!

The Ultimate "Body of Christ"

Next, the digital environment is a community environment:

> The true value of a network is less about information and more about community. The information superhighway is more than a short cut to every book in the Library of Congress. It is creating a totally new, global social fabric.[18]

After all, the computer communicates, and its communication creates community. In this community, a "harmonizing web" of individuals join in common interests to form intricate networks of interaction and interdependency. If we could "see" cyberspace, it would look like a "knotted fish net with a multitude of nodes of varying sizes, each linked to all the others, directly or indirectly."[19]

But this is a new community . . . a new affinity group. It is a distal community that transcends distance. It is an environment without an environment. It is a new generation released from the limits of nearness as the sole basis for friendship, teamwork, play, and neighborhood.[20]

It also has a new global speech. "English will be the de facto air-traffic-control-type language."[21] And, even with foreign tongues, the language of currency will remain universal "bits." Or, applying church metaphors to the secular economy, Don Tapscott writes, "Everybody can use the same hymn book."

And finally, this affinity group is a new family. "In its rich opportunities for mutual aid and support, the network is reminiscent of its forebear, the kinship system. Yet, this 'family' has formed from deeply held values and shared assumptions, bonds thicker than blood."[22]

Answering those who believe the computer will destroy community, Negroponte says, "It's just going to make the community circle a much tighter circle in both senses of the word: tighter in terms of bond and tighter in terms of a smaller circle.'"[23] Riel Miller asserts, "It will be an age of 'in your face' contact harkening back to village life."[24] And Tapscott writes, "Unlike the Walkman, a technological revolution that created isolation, the next wave will be all about community, communications, and sharing what we know."[25]

Of course, the Church *is* community. Wherever hearts unite under the Lordship of Christ, we find the Church. But this is a new church . . . a Cyber church—a sacred culture of telecommunications. Like the new paradigm church LaMar Boschman describes, "It links in like-minded networks through a *spiritual* bond, rather than an organizational or legal bond."[26]

Then, in the truest sense of Paul's famous phrase, this spiritual bond becomes the ultimate "Body of Christ." The Internet is like an "extension of the central nervous system . . . connecting the various parts of the body."[27] And when all the world's computers unite, the network itself becomes a giant computer, infinitely more powerful than any individual. In other words, this extended "body" creates a synergistic force where "two or more come together to achieve an effect of which each alone is incapable."

Paul would have been thrilled! The Church Universal is no longer an abstract idea.

"Power in New Hands"

Finally, the digital age proclaims a new freedom and a new empowerment. The church has suffered hidden tyrannies for years, but now, the door opens to a new liberty and a new latitude. The church is not only free *from* something, but free *for* something.

Here is an example of what it is freed from:

In the Holy Roman Empire, the role of clergy grew strong, central, and unquestioned. It was a high-status role carrying total authority. "Rector," for example, meant "ruler." And the remaining church history—Protestant history included—reveals the same dreary story. "During a thousand years of Christendom the churches built a power system controlled by the clergy—a clericalism that now distorts power relationships."[28]

Why? Because command-and-control hierarchies tend to concentrate power at the top. Institutional liaisons easily become fraternities of forensics. Elite clerical castes often harbor illusions of professional spirituality. And authoritarian power brokers usually manipulate their programs of vested interests.

All this, of course, is the antithesis of Christianity.

It is also the antithesis of the digital age. "Computer technology is profoundly anti-authoritarian."[29] Already its insurrection appears in the new economy, for "the firm as we know it is breaking up."[30] The old top-down model is long past. Negroponte puts it this way:

The so-called management information systems (MIS) czar, who used to reign over a glass-enclosed and air-conditioned mausoleum, is an emperor with

no clothes, almost extinct . . . The traditional cen-
tralist view of life will become a thing of the past.[31]

History will see, instead, a "monumental reallocation of
power,"[32] and it is reallocating to the grassroots. Nobody owns the
Net, for example; everyone owns it. It is a truly open system where
all users have a say—even the poor. In fact, the fastest growing
numbers of Internet hosts appear in third world countries like
Slovenia, Indonesia, Iran, Peru. . . .[33]

But their power is a different power. Big is no longer better.
The smallest groups can change society by simply combining their
knowledge and creativity. And nothing can stop them. Today, no
governing bodies oversee the Internet—nor can they oversee it. For
the united forces of technology and human nature will always prove
stronger. As Internet pioneer John Gilmore puts it, "The Net
interprets censorship as damage and routes around it."

Of course, all this freedom and power bring with it a new
laity. They have discovered that the Church is for them and not the
presbytery. Pollster George Gallup reports:

> Unlike any decade in history that preceded it, the
> decade of the 1990's will be shaped by the people
> themselves . . . from the bottom up . . . We will hear
> a more persistent voice from the laity, who want a
> greater role in shaping the church.[34]

Or, echoing Luther, the liberty and ability to witness
worldwide at the speed of light—and with the Spirit of light—is
creating a new "priesthood of believers." It's strange how this shift
in power will prove—in the same moment—both the demise and
the salvation of the church as we know it.

Just Creativity and Sand

But this salvation includes still other forms of freedoms and empowerments: No longer will money be an issue. No longer will buildings, broadcasts, wages, mailings and other outlays be burdens. For "human capital has replaced dollar capital."[35]

Fifteen years ago, for example, Microsoft had almost no capital. Now—with ideas alone—its share of wealth grows greater than either General Motors or IBM.

This empowerment means the church can also do more with less. It will run world missions once requiring vast resources. Tomorrow, for example, capital driven mega-ministries must compete with small—yet equally powerful—"cottage" ministries.

Replacing old drivers of success (capital assets, mass media, and clerical armies) a new laity will charge the front line with nothing but cheap and endless supplies of creativity and "sand."

(Note: The silicon of computers and the glass fibers of telecommunications are mere sand).

Images and Enemies

And no longer will the church suffer image problems . . . the disaffection of dead doctrines . . . the alienation of empty ethics . . . the apathy of temporal pursuits . . . or the hostility of honed hatreds. For in cyberspace, "it is difficult to distinguish between insider and outsider, between members of the family and those who are 'just visiting'."[36] A famous cartoon says it all: Two dogs are using the Internet . . . one dog types to the other: "On the Internet, nobody knows you're a dog."

So the church can assume any mode, manner, or medium it wants to assume. It can move incognito through space and time. It can trap unsuspecting iniquity in the mighty arms of its grace.

Even its most vengeful (and powerful) secular enemies—often the mass media—can be overcome. First, "Church concerns cannot be silenced (on the Internet) as easily as they can in other media."[37] But more important, media giants will command no advantage, because the church will also publish—"on-line" . . . with no paper costs . . . no printing costs . . . and no postage costs. In fact, on the Internet, each church can be an unlicensed TV station, broadcasting worldwide with both video and sound.

That's not all. The church will fly in the face of any political or cultural censors that lie behind forbidden boundaries. No one will stop its irrepressible message any more than the Romans stopped Christianity.

———————— •••◦●◦•• ————————

The coming age holds unimaginable opportunity for the church, for the world will be conquered by the next collective, networked, virtual force that flows from a jointly created, shared vision. And this force can be the Church! It is our one—and maybe last—chance. We can't go backwards. "If we had to restructure a society with the old tactics, it would seem a hopelessly large task, like reversing the spin of the planet."[38]

Yet, looking ahead, we need not fear. Even if French philosopher Jacques Ellul believes the world will self-destruct,[39] the Church is *not* the world. The Church has no reason to become victim to the world.

For "where sin abounded, grace did much more abound."[40]

5. "ONCE MORE WITH FEELING"

"No Hugs and Kisses"

The way the world communicates filters and fashions its message. The medium it uses, in other words, shapes the content of the message . . . even the way one thinks. Whether society builds cars or cultures, its tools bias the results.

Other than the purest saints, believers can't see this bias. Like the air one breathes, the multitudes move within these media. And when the medium changes . . . the church changes.

History has known three main media: the oral tradition—symbolized by speech, the print medium—embodied by books, and the electronic age—taken over by TV. Now, again, we brave the trauma of still another medium . . . another environment . . . another reality.

The digital age.

"In the beginning . . . God said. . . ." And that was enough! From then on, *words were power* . . . at least, until the print and electronic media came along. Then, words turned morally deficient. The age of print became "law without life," the age of TV became "life without law."[1] Both "have a form of godliness, but deny the power thereof."[2]

Now, similar doubts defy the digital age. Skeptics call the Internet, for example, "unreal" and "impersonal." After all, they say, "There are no hugs and kisses. Digitized sight and sound—or any other sensations—are not real! They are only bytes and bits . . . a series of yes/noes or dot/dashes . . . data without meaning."

Kissed Nevertheless

But trends tell of a digital age more personal than imagined. The *real* digital age—just around the corner—will be both high tech and high touch . . . "aesthetic qualities and technical excellence . . . style and content . . . meaning and performance."[3] Already the theologian Lochhead witnesses:

> Surprisingly, (computer relationships) are very personal . . . intense . . . warm . . . intimate . . . (They are a) highly-charged medium emotionally . . . In our on-line communities we have seen many surprising examples of intimacy, love, and caring . . . a community where people laugh and cry, where tenderness and anger both are powerfully conveyed.[4]

And computer expert Negroponte foresees even more cosmic affections. Virtual reality "will allow you to put your arms around the Milky Way, swim in the human bloodstream, or visit Alice in Wonderland."[5]

Silly? No!

The collusion of head and heart will prove self-evident when full-scale multimedia invade our homes. Until now, physical contact has been stripped away. Sensuous computing has merely placed second to getting kissed over the phone! But soon, multimedia will satiate our sensory needs. As audio, image, video—and other sensory images—become evermore blended, personal computers will become evermore personal.

Already, we savor these digital deeps. Beethoven's music loses nothing when the coded data of a CD turns soul into sound.

In fact, CD's surpass even live concerts when poor acoustics impair our hearing. That's because

> All music is what awakes from you when you are
>   reminded by the instruments,
> It is not the violins and the cornets, it is not the oboe
>   nor the beating drums, nor the score of the baritone
>   singer who singing his sweet romanza, nor that of
>   the men's chorus, nor that of the women's chorus,
>   [nor the bytes and bits of computer codes!],
> It is nearer and farther than they.[6]

Back to the Past

In reality, the coming digital age proves not only personal, it proves a probable return, to the "Word" of the first century—the oral medium. Like the stage-play title, "Once More with Feeling," we will return, in many ways, to the oral tradition.

This may prove true. Read on!

Was the oral medium intimate? So is the growing multimedia, multisensory world. Was early speech one-on-one? So is a new "de-massified" . . . "on-line" . . . "in-your-face" future. Was there equal access in early dialogue? So is there equal access in the new dialogue.

Did the oral culture nurture meditation? So do enhanced mixtures of high tech and hypertext. Did ancient prophets share inspired visions? So do our intuitive cyber-prophets. Did knowledge move through sacraments and symbols? So do today's data move through super-symbolic cyberspace.

Do we recall shared memories of sacred sages? So shall we
share memories of the greatest ages. Do we recall powerful
moments in ancient life? So shall we know real-time events in
future life. Do we recall godly Words of eternal and universal
significance? So shall we summon global "words" of timeless and
spaceless transcendence.

Whether these comparisons seem exact, or inexact, makes
no difference. Such abundant coincidence cannot be denied.

Neither Binary Digits nor Balaam's Donkey

Yet, such coincidence means nothing unless future believers
understand the "Words" in oral words. That is . . . until they
understand what "communicates" in oral communication.

Our cognitive culture deceives itself with literal "words,"
and we delude ourselves with their literal meanings. The bytes and
bits in computer files, for example, may be reality, and they may
form literal "words," but they are not the message. And—at the
deepest level—they are not even the medium.

A true "Word"—an oral word—does not limit itself to mere
"information." It speaks, instead, a specific message to a specific
person at a specific time. It entices with sudden notice. It attracts
with something beyond the "word" itself. It lures with something
very desirable . . . attractive . . . meaningful.

And great thinkers agree this attraction proves its own truth.

Neither does the "Word" of the oral medium limit itself to
the "spoken" word. It comes, instead, as a direct, intuitive revelation. It is written, Paul said, "with the Spirit of the living God . . .
(on) human hearts."[7]

Granted, the digital medium brings a different "word" . . .
a new "word"—"linking concepts to one another in startling ways
. . . building up amazing hierarchies of inference . . . spawning new
theories, hypotheses and images based on novel assumptions . . .
(and developing) new languages, codes and logics."[8] But the
ancient oral "Word" will transcend even this new medium.

As Negroponte points out, "Surely, the 'real thing' is not an
expression of itself, but is itself."[9]

So it doesn't matter whether the medium is binary digits or
Balaam's donkey,[10] God speaks through them anyway. For a true
"Word" is any place where Spirit speaks to spirit. It is any medium
where Spirit takes on body and body takes on Spirit.

A Multisensory Hall of Mirrors

Let's compare more closely the ancient oral tradition and the
new digital medium.

As mentioned earlier, the oral world is a personal world. It
provides firsthand experience . . . with senses and feelings . . .
intensity and immediacy. For example, the ancient—but highly
sensory—metaphor provided not only the primary voice in the oral
medium, but the primary art as well. In fact, the rules of this
primitive metaphor provide a perfect model for all the arts . . . any
time, any place.[11]

But the coming digital age will prove highly sensory as well.
Its multimedia, multisensory, multimodal "words" will supercharge
the senses. "It's not unthinkable that smell and even taste will be
integrated into the . . . experience."[12] Already computers provide
kinesthetic feelings (the sense of movement, whether we are
moving or not). We find these feelings when flight simulators

generate genuine interactivity, 3D maneuvers, real-time animation, and photorealism.[13]

In truth, digital sensory images will become so abundant and vivid that participants will find it hard to free themselves from such a beguiling embrace. Right or wrong, these images will drive the future.

But these supercharged senses will do more than drive twenty-first century video games. For a new "knowing" emotion will compel a new "knowledge." William Irwin Thompson already sees it occurring:

> As fiction and music are coming close to reorganiz-
> ing knowledge, scholarship is becoming closer to art
> . . . in our electronic, cybernetic society, the genre is
> *Wissenkunst*: the play of knowledge in a world of
> serious data-processors . . . At such a moment as
> this the novelist becomes a prophet, the composer a
> magician, and the historian a bard, a voice recalling
> ancient identities.[14]

In short, the digital age will blend the technical and the tasteful . . . the scientific and the aesthetic . . . the left brain and the right brain . . . the message and the meaning. For "mathematical statistics and poetry alike . . . reduce to a digital stream."[15]

(The Greek *techna*—from which we derive "technol-ogy"—finally makes sense! It means "art"!)

Strange as it may seem, music—with its intrinsic math—may prove the primary symbol in the digital age. "Music has proven to be one of the most important shaping forces in computer science . . . (a) perfect intellectual landscape for moving gracefully between technology and expression, science and art, private and public."[16]

Yet, the emphasis will remain multimedia—mixing audio, video, data, and more . . . culling meaning from many concurrent channels of communication . . . from many dissimilar sensory sources. And these potent mixtures will prove no ordinary multimedia events. In fact, they will surpass any multimedia of the past and totally change the media landscape of the future. Already, "Whole new art forms are emerging based on multimedia."[17]

Why? Because computer bits merge and mix easily. They flow freely from one medium to the other . . . from one sense to the other. They easily imitate our ability to imagine one notion for another. When, for example, a soprano sings with a "bright voice," we replace sound with sight. In the same way, computers will mirror one feeling for another. They will reflect one sense for another.

And in this virtual hall of mirrors, new multisensory media will build ever deeper metaphors of metaphors.

Breaking the Boundaries of Belief

Continuing these comparisons, consider another major theme of the oral environment: It pushes the boundary of belief. It proclaims impossible promises . . . it heralds a hidden future . . . it declares deeds already done that are still undone.

In the words of Scripture, it "calls those things that be not as though they were."[18]

The Bible, for example, does not describe what is. It describes, instead, what is coming to be. Faith itself expects the

yet-to-be. It looks "to things that are unseen" and "perceives" the
things hoped for. Then it gives "substance" to this vision.[19]

But notice. The same paradox between "what is" and "what
is not" appears in "virtual reality." This new mania presents "a
world in which the clear borderlines between the real and the
possible, between work and play, between here and there, are no
longer present."[20] It simulates sense experiences so palpable . . . so
immediate . . . so convincing that they are called "real"—though
still unreal!

It's been said, "If prizes are awarded for the best
oxymorons, 'virtual reality' would certainly be a winner."[21] As a
result, this digital paradox shares the same prophetic vision—that
is, breaks the same belief barriers—as the oral medium. And
churches who learn how to use "virtual reality" for sacred purposes
can find a new and powerful art form.

Raw forms of virtual reality appeared first in "B" movies,
but soon found lofty refinement in flight simulation. Indeed, virtual
reality is now state-of-the-art. As example, Douglas Trumbull—the
special effects wizard in *Close Encounters of the Third
Kind*—designed a theater at the Las Vegas Luxor Casino that
actually transports audiences into another reality . . . into visionary
realms seen as real events.

Trumball calls it "an experiment in finally going over the
edge of a belief barrier."[22]

In short, virtual reality will fully copy reality with an awe-
inspiring array of limitless, lifelike experiences. And, yes, it will be
misused. It will be burdened with "vain imaginings"—godless
delusions, empty schemes, malicious caprice. More than ever, God
will test us . . . as we "test the spirits"![23] Then He will expect us to
refuse these "vain imaginings."[24]

Still, the Church can harness the prophetic potential of this new science. It can model a godly vision in future time. It can meditate metaphors of a virtual spirit realm . . . of a foreseen vision of truth. It can make the intangible tangible . . . the invisible visible . . . the implicit explicit.

This opportunity differs in no way, after all, from the prophetic revelations of ancient Scripture where—even today—beautiful visions still capture hungry hearts. Nor does virtual reality differ from familiar art forms, rituals, or symbols. All of them can represent things "not seen." All of them can point beyond themselves . . can transform us . . . recreate us . . . heal us.

Images on Top of Images

History will reveal yet another parallel between the ancient oral tradition and the new digital medium. It will mirror the "meditation" of an ancient communion and the "interaction" of a future interface. In both, we will receive, then respond . . . contemplate, then participate.

Negroponte calls the digital version a "multimodal interface."[25] But Thompson simply calls it what it is . . . a "culture of meditation"[26] Again, this is a return to the ancient past.

Let's look first at the ancient version.

Oral "meditation" explains itself when linking its original meaning with its Scriptural context. Here is a summary: "Judeo-Christian meditation contemplates things of the spirit and reflects the resulting visions in a dialogue with God." Or—for our purpose—"Meditative visions speak through *inspired sensory images and feelings* that at first may not be clear to the natural mind."

Plainly, this reflective dialogue created a virtual Hebrew "hall of mirrors." And this mirroring presented, as well, a perfect model for the prophetic artist. For the "doing" of meditation coincided with creativity and usually led to a work of art: parables, proverbs, stories, songs, the sounds of musical instruments, and other artistic forms.

In the digital world, there is similar dialogue . . . similar interactivity . . . similar "symbolic processing"[27] . . . similar creative innovation. The Internet, after all, is a realm of interaction and interdependency . . . a place where insights are linked and networked. Truly, its real-time, virtual environment inspires interactivity.

. . . even creativity! For its symbolic processing culls meaning from many different, yet concurrent, channels of communication. Through inference, context, and analogy, it piles assumptions on top of assumptions . . . images on top of images . . . insights on top of insights.

"Hypertext" serves as an example:

> (In) hypertext, a term for highly interconnected narrative, or linked information . . . an expression of an idea or train of thought can include a multidimensional network of pointers to further elaborations or arguments, which can be invoked or ignored . . . Chunks of information can be reordered, sentences expanded, and words given definitions on the spot . . . elastic messages can stretch and shrink in accordance with the reader's actions. Ideas can be opened and analyzed at multiple levels of detail . . . like barbershop mirrors, an image within an image within an image.[28]

But the future promises even more power, for the new multimedia will blend space-age technique with ancient-age artistry. It will shock the observer with the shared meanings of different modes, moods, senses, and scenes.

The "hologram" proves a perfect example: In this three-dimension photo, each part presents the whole picture while highlighting—at the same time—a different view. Take a holographic picture, for example, of a full symphony orchestra . . . remove the trumpet . . . then shine a laser beam through only the trumpet, and the entire orchestra will be recreated!

What an exciting time for the children of a Creator-God! David Ticoll, of the Alliance for Converging Technologies, promises "intuition and creativity will blossom in . . . the fertile soil of the new media." Yet, years ago, Albert Einstein saw the fruit of this future when he said, "Imagination is more important than knowledge."

The story *Through the Looking-Glass* by Lewis Carrol comes close to these New Millennium truths, for it was "through a mirror" that "Alice" entered the "other world." In the same way, it will be through reflective meditation we will enter the new world. I believe that's the reason Tal Brooke calls the Internet an "electronic mirror."[29]

> "We all, with uncovered face, reflecting as in a mirror the glory of the Lord, are having our outward expressions changed into the same image from one degree of glory to another."[30]

Ancient Kinships

Futurists will find one final—and surprising—return to the oral age: One-on-one relations. Why surprising? Because the mass media have disembodied and disempowered the individual.

And many observers say the future fares no better. Rather than "high-tech, high-touch," these cynics expect only "high-tech, out-of-touch."[31] Yet, already mass communications are things of the past. Already "Broadcasting and the mass media are in their final days."[32] No longer are consumers simply "faces in the crowd."

We have passed into a "post-mass-media" age where the audience is often the size of one—where everything is made to order . . . extremely personalized . . . endlessly customized.

After all,

I am *me*, not a statistical subset . . . Classic demo-
graphics do not scale down to the digital individual
. . . (for the digital age) is based on a model of you
as an individual, not as part of a group.[33]

As a result, advertisers are targeting smaller and smaller market segments to reach dissimilar customers with greater precision. The "intimate relationship between producer and consumer . . . will shatter the anonymity of mass consumption, mass politics, mass media. It will be an age of 'in your face' contact harkening back to village life."[34]

And in this village, a modern version of ancient kinship will appear. For on the Internet, each member is at the center and the center is everywhere.[35] After all, if the digital age has any ethics at all, it's this: "Access and equity should be unlimited and total." So no one will be left out! Given a will, gaps will be reduced, not increased.

Churches are reflecting the same trends. Micro-churches are replacing mega-churches. Smaller, intimate churches—like those of early Christianity—are replacing anonymous, faceless institutions. Informal, low-tech, oral media are replacing controlled, show business, mass productions.

International worship leader LaMar Boschman reports, for example, that the cutting edge churches of the world are dropping all labels . . . all classifications . . . anything that abandons believers to a faceless crowd. He illustrates further the rapidly growing "house church" in China where the saved are discipled for three years and then sent out to start another church.[36]

But the digital age adds an amazing touch to this change. Consider the history: The early church grew "one-on-one." Though heroic, its actions were limiting, time-consuming, and dangerous. Then the Roman Empire turned this faith into a state religion . . . a faceless, government-endorsed mission to conquer the known world. Now—for the first time—the church can be both large and small . . . both global and personal.

All in the same moment!

In honesty, information technology—on its own—will not build the Kingdom. Nevertheless, a prophetic Church will surely show signs of the Kingdom.

Maranatha!

III. THE IMPERATIVE

6. EATING ELEPHANTS

Ends and Means

Yes, God is sovereign. He always wins. But when the church fails to see what God is doing in history and refuses to follow His lead, it suffers the result. History repeatedly proves this. Yet, the church has no plan for the digital age. Experts inundate clerics with the latest ideals for current culture, but few put forward a plan for future culture.

The church was never called to follow society rather than lead society. The church was never asked to separate ends from means—to simply hope somehow to get from here to there. On the contrary, Christianity always activates its faith. It always models its love. It always mixes method with its mission.

After all, God is not a passive Spirit. His presence in history surpasses mere theology. He moves in the middle of the raw and real. Yet, the raw and real are listening less and less to the church.

Today—as yesterday—Jesus calls out: "Interpret the signs of the times"![37]

"Born in Another Time"

Interpreting these signs, leaders must step outside their box . . . check their assumptions . . . be open to new ideas . . . get curious . . . grow sensitive to trends and events . . . and, like theologian Lochhead, ask questions:

> What do we mean 'proclamation' in a medium that is essentially dialogical? What is 'mission' in an electronic community? Is worship possible on-line? In an information society, what is the place of a community like the church which values wisdom more than it values data?[1]

Of course, answers to questions like these require different ways of thinking. Yes, God's Word always remains the same, but a new paradigm demands new understandings. And—in the digital paradigm—those new understandings demand intuitive insights, hypertext perceptions, feeling phenomena, metaphoric meanings. . . .

Old analytic ways—step by step thoughts—can no longer plod along. For today's instant facts coexist in an active interplay . . . the newest data is suddenly done in by even newer data. And old realities—the material world itself—can no longer rule every plan. For the atoms of material commerce are being replaced by the "bytes" of immaterial barter—both weightless and "waitless."

The church does not have to choose between God's Kingdom and these changing realities. Spiritual depth and worldly breadth are not either/or. The church must discern the values of secular knowledge . . . learn the trends of the times . . . and use that which best manifests its mission.

Then finally, the Church must raise this awareness in others. It must empower grass-root leaders with the same vision. It must turn freedom of information into freedom of spirit. It must translate secular information into worldly knowledge and worldly knowledge into prophetic wisdom.

"Do not confine your children to
your own learning, for they were
born in another time."[2]

Riding Waves and Measuring Undercurrents

So leaders must clearly understand this cultural moment . .
. where we are, how we got here, and where we're going.

The church must learn to see both the comprehensive and
the particular . . . vistas and vignettes . . . reality and facts. It must
learn to envision the dusk and dawn of a single horizon, yet walk in
the noonday sun. It must learn to soar above the complexity to the
whole, yet plunge below the complexity to the core. It must ride the
waves of a vast ocean, yet measure the speed and direction of the
undercurrents.

More than mere survival, good reasons exist for this
understanding. Tapscott writes, "An expert is a person who simply
keeps up because knowledge doubles every 18 months." So the
church needs a running start just to keep up!

In the global economy, for example, knowledge has become
the only basis of value—Peter Drucker reports—the only meaningful resource. If this is true for business, how much more so for the
church! Let it remember the sons of Issachar:

. . . men who had understanding of the times to
know what Israel ought to do.[3]

"Just do it!"

The church can't wait until forced into action. The promised land is now. After all, Christian love is active, not passive. It

always purposes itself toward the world. It always fulfills the Father's will in the world.

Advanced electronic media in the hands of bankrupt spirits will soon destroy us. And—at the moment—bankrupt spirits rule the day. Of the four worldwide religious forces that can drive the digital age—Christianity, Islam, humanism, and the New Age—the New Age is manifestly evident. This postmodern, post-Christian movement now serves as the unspoken religion of the Information Age, and it often stands overtly hostile to Christianity.

Countless New Age teachers and spiritual leaders are moving across cultural boundaries. They claim, "Nothing is forbidden."

Solzhenitsyn sees the threat:

Destructive and irresponsible freedom has been granted boundless space . . . (with) little defense against the abyss of human decadence . . . (with an) inability to defend itself against the corrosion of evil. . . . Such a tilt of freedom in the direction of evil has come about . . . (with the idea) there is no evil inherent in human nature.[4]

As a result, the Internet harbors a darker side to cyberspace. It parades a rapidly expanding ghetto of depravity.

A case in point:

Wired editor Eric Davis names a leading cyber-whiz who "practices witchcraft and coordinates a Bay area coven of fellow software and hardware cutting-edge innovators. This digital age guru describes himself as a 'gay witch'," yet his creations have become "a technical standard for the World Wide Web."[5]

Still, in the face of threats like these, the church remains
oblivious to its enemies. Surely we must begin to grasp that "It's
now a battle for the entire planet's faith."[6]

> "We must get our act together and
> prepare the church for action or suf-
> fer badly for our unwillingness to
> discern God's hand in this karios."[7]

One "Byte" at a Time

"Getting our act together" first requires fluency in the digital
medium. This fluency should become our intuitive nature . . . our
second language. In the old mass media paradigm, only the
broadcasters needed to understand their medium. Now everyone
needs these skills.

Especially a prophetic Church.

Rex Miller compares this discipline to the creative fluency
of great artists. Artists do not take their medium for granted.
Whether working with canvass, cinema, clay, or anything else, they
know that each medium carries peculiar qualities . . . each skill
prescribes strict boundaries; and artists soon discover and respect
both the limits and potential of their craft.[8]

All this requires moving quickly . . . yet taking one step at
a time. The church needs thousands of "safe" experiments that
prototype the future. (The reader will find a summary of these
experiments in the last chapter of this book.) Whatever the attempt,
these efforts must gestate long enough to accommodate success.

There's proof in this prudence . . . security in this safety.
Alvin Toffler says the global race will be won by groups complet-

ing their transformation with the least amount of dislocation and unrest.[9]

It's a mammoth task. So we must eat this elephant one "byte" at a time.

> "Churches must learn to encourage innovation and even fund it . . . In times and places where change is rapid, our most important asset is the pioneer, the one—or the many—who is willing to break new paths."[10]

7. DYING TO LIVE

Meaningless Martyrdoms

The church must die to live. It must decease to receive. It must let go of old paradigms to embrace new paradigms.

Tragically, ensconced leaders are often the last to welcome this truth. They paid heavily for their positions and resist all attempts to change them. They've gained from past largess and oppose all threats to its sweetness.

So they simply dig in their heels. With old and impotent models, these guardians expend their "resources and energy in shoring up collapsing structures." They hold "onto the familiar long after it has lost its possibility for new life."[1]

When the truth finally breaks their beloved illusions, they react as with real death. Initially, they show denial (they continue as if nothing has happened) . . . then depression (they become tired, listless) . . . then a zeal for bargains (they latch onto anything that will turn the clock back) . . . and, finally, anger (they blame others.)[2]

To avoid meaningless martyrdoms, leaders must crucify these hidden tyrannies. The apostle James said, "If anyone thinks himself to be religious . . . but deludes his own heart, this person's religious service is worthless."[3]

Breaking Balloons

So, first, die to irrelevance. History overflows with spiritual movements that provided fresh insight for a moment only to be swept away by obsolescence in the next moment. When an entire sector of the population doesn't listen to the church anymore, it's time to get relevant.

This means, for example, dropping religious jargon, in-house codes, meaningless metaphors, and archaic styles. After all, in the old King James English, one could just as well say "thou" to a prostitute and "thee" to a bartender.

God is not impressed.

Next, die to self-satisfaction . . . the cozy comforts of proud pieties. Like looking into mirrors, some congregations worship their own worship. They turn it into a fetish—an object of its own awe.

We choose churches, for example, from whatever affirms us, entertains us, satisfies us, or makes us feel good about God and ourselves.[4] In truth, the fantasies of our cherished choices "make (us) feel good because they are in harmony with (our) opinions, prejudices, and unconscious assumptions about the nature of reality."[5]

In other words, we scratch our own itch!

Next, die to worn-out traditions. Religious traditions are simply ways the gospel speaks in specific historical moments. Yet, these myopic moments are too often set apart as sacraments themselves.

When traditions turn to hollow ritual, impotent style, dead orthodoxy, or mute relics . . . when they become old and stale, like bread left out overnight . . . when they stand mired in the past, like ruins of an ancient culture . . . they need to be lovingly laid to rest.

The conductor Toscanini offered a musical reminder, "Tradition is the last bad concert."

Citizen Souls

All these illusions mean dying to the "institutional" church—"the self-imposed codes of an entrenched religious culture."[6]

The class in power, by secular definition, prescribes politically correct rules and then canonizes them within a closed system. This definition also describes the "established" church. It is, after all, a relentless relic of the Holy Roman Empire where "citizen souls" were "saved" by the Empire.

Sally Morgenthaler calls this "churchianity." But, in truth, it is called "religion."

In its purest form, Christianity was always anti-establishment . . . counter-cultural . . . at odds with the world's view. That's why Jeremiah called our trust in outward forms of religion—in place of inward bonds to the Lord—"deceptive." He proclaimed, instead, a "new covenant" written on the heart.[7]

Contrary to opinion, the institutional church was never a "universal" Church. Even the Reformation continues to splinter into a dizzying variety of creeds. Paraphrasing Paul, "The Messiah has been chopped up in little pieces so we can each have a relic all our own."[8]

Worst of all, the aspiring priests of these worldly theocracies lift themselves to God, believing He will approve their wonderful efforts. But their ascent shows an innocent deceit: presuming God's presence *by* worship rather than *with* worship.

They seem to forget that Jesus came down to *where* we are . . . met us *as* we are.

So the institutional church carries too much baggage. It should begin by dropping its labels and titles, for the world will come to the Church only if it is not *for* the "church." Just as health is more than medicine and learning more than education, spirituality is more than religion.

Flexible Hearts

Whether following or being followed, both believers and leaders must live ongoing redemptions. Dying is not a one-time event. Paul said, "I die daily!"[9] So a true church always creatively destructs . . . continuously unlearns.

Scripture documents these deaths. The bronze serpent, created by Moses at the Lord's command, eventually had to be destroyed. The ark of the covenant finally disappeared, and Solomon's temple, which became a talisman of God's protection, was later demolished.

The modern church is no different. The Pope's *Constitution on the Sacred Liturgy* admits some things are "subject to change" and require adapting to the needs of the times.[10] Of, course, the follow-up to his vision has proven more difficult.

Church leaders should not fret. This death is not a breakdown. It's a breakthrough!

In truth, this "unlearning" . . . this "dying" is more than gospel. It is, in fact, a practical necessity! Creative stress always transforms the future. And today, history requires it more than ever, for the world is changing—it is in a fluid state. The past no longer certifies the future, so we must cooperate with this change.

After all, Christianity is not a status, but a journey. Paul paraphrases God's prophetic voice: "I'll turn conventional wisdom on its head, I'll expose so-called experts as crackpots." And Jesus adds, "I prefer a flexible heart to an inflexible ritual."[11]

> "Finding paths into the past is such
> a luxury, finding them for the future
> such a burden."[12]

8. TURNING THE CHURCH UPSIDE-DOWN

New Patterns of Peers

When the way we communicate changes, the way we wield power changes. In other words, a new medium births a new polity . . . a new communication aligns a new power. Just as the printing press broke past political structures, the digital age will break present political structures.

It will reapportion power on a massive scale.

Global business already senses this shift. In fact, the search is on for new alliances of authority, new systems of influence, new patterns of peers, and what they find will turn the church upside-down!

Why? Because a digital society is totally anti-authority. Its diversity blows the circuits of central power. And its self-sufficiency easily survives censorship.

Decentralizing will prove its ultimate triumph.[1]

This means future leaders will learn a "non-local" polity . . . a "non-territorial" alliance. They will learn facilitator skills . . . shared powers that expand. And church leaders will learn—as the early Quakers did—a new reliance on the Holy Spirit . . . a free and formless "control."

In short, they will learn that Jesus is "in the *midst* of the congregation"—not on the platform![2]

Historian Alvin Toffler describes this radical change:

(These) forces in America have yet to find their
voice. The (movement) that gives it to them will
dominate the American future . . . Movements that
recognize this historical fact will survive and shape
the future for our children. Those that fail to do so
will swirl down the storm drain of history.[3]

The Emperor with No Clothes

Successful companies already see the breakup of old top-
down, centralized, command-and-control bureaucracies. Global
entrepreneurs already experience the dethronement of old mono-
lithic, hierarchic, and autocratic empires.

Bigger is not always better.

In the first place, rigid old models become unwieldy in the
complexity of the new world. Over-centralized decisions become
"decision overload" in the rapidity of a real-time environment. And
huge offices and expensive overheads become competitive
disasters.

Why? Because power at the top nearly always focuses on
itself. Vested interests and the struggle for security conspire for the
ease and pleasure of those in charge.

Always subtle, always there.

And egocentric power always pushes one way—downward.
Whether manipulating, exploiting, care-taking, or battling, the top
always assumes power over the bottom. It's a win/lose posture that

cuts off promises from below, for the order of the day is conformity—no opinion, no dissent.

It's an old world of aggressive leaders and passive followers. Yet, the so-called management czar "is an emperor with no clothes, almost extinct."[4]

Surrogate Worship

This emperor also approaches extinction in the church, but he doesn't know it.

An elite priestly caste still operates out of the old school. "Professionals" of the spirit . . . brokers of power . . . manipulators of programs.

All too frequently, they *are* the ministry!

They divide the body of Christ into overworked leaders and sedentary serfs. They convince the laity to relinquish their priesthood to professionals. They protect the insulating gap between assuredly strong leaders and obviously weak followers.

These are wise shepherds . . . the others, dumb lambs.

Of course, such hierarchy only works with micro-management—when the top monitors all the functions. So assignments and protocol for mission stand as the paid officials define them . . . as the institutions demand them.

Individual gifts only muddy up the water.

In today's mega-churches, for example, leaders slip easily into pastor-centered ministries . . . high profile personalities . . . and even show-business celebrities. In short, their ministries become personality cults. Then, of course, hype, manipulation, and church "groupies" follow closely behind.

But there's a price to pay. While the professionals up front "perform" worship the followers out front resign themselves to spectators . . . passive observers . . . "trainee mutes" . . . "pew potatoes."

At best, it's a surrogate worship. The success of the service depends entirely on "how well the minister did."

And the rest of the church "programs" follow suit.

Brooks Brothers' Suits

How did the lessons of history vanish so quickly?

When Christianity became the official religion of the Roman Empire, the bishop moved his seat from among the people to the altar. It became the place of honor, power . . . and later the throne. Then gradually the clergy even removed worship from the people and kept it for themselves. . . .

. . . while the people watched.

Later, the Reformation merely exchanged the priest for a minister and put a sermon in place of communion. Then, the rest of history simply supported these distortions. The Enlightenment turned preaching into worship, and modern management turned preachers into executives.

Today, too many priests of Christendom wear Brooks Brothers' suits.

How tragic! None of these things trace to Christian origins. Indeed, authoritarian rule and blind passivity go against the very foundations of Christianity. The idea that "laity" somehow differ from "clergy" is unscriptural. For the "laity" in the ancient Greek "are in the same ballpark as peon, peasant, amateur, yokel, and the great unwashed."[5]

Even the hierarchical "church" in our Bibles is an idea preferred "by King James, who for political reasons *ordered* his translators to use (the word "church") rather than the more obvious 'assembly' or 'gathering'."[6] Of course, the latter terms suggests a less structured, less controlled, less monarchical crowd, and King James knew this.

While "successful" clergy maneuver for reputations, we must remember that Jesus "made Himself of no reputation."[7] He stripped Himself of all privileges and rightful dignity so He could assume the guise of a servant.

> "The old model of oversight will not be adequate. In many places even today it is in crisis or collapse already."[8]

A New "Priesthood of Believers"

All the church surveys say members born after 1965 have a hostility toward hierarchy. They detest being "owned" like employees. They don't like being told what to do by paid officials.

Instead, they want to be released and empowered to find their own voice . . . to initiate their own ideas . . . to shape and mold their own mission. Yet, they want to do it as part of a team . . . serving a broader context . . . working with a larger family.

And their vision has arrived! For the digital age is a grassroots phenomenon . . . a great leveler. It will empower a new laity. It will pioneer a new "priesthood of believers."

Because churches surviving in the future will decentralize . . . their control will broaden. No longer will information simply be "pushed down" from the top. The believers at the bottom will also "pull down" the information they need—on demand data . . . for specific purposes . . . at specific times . . . and in specific places.

And everyone will participate. For the new medium does not require great wealth, staff, buildings, resources, or reputations. Indeed, the digital age will allow individuals to create solutions that rival those of vast corporations.

In the future, "big" will no longer intimidate!

For the computer puts power in the hands of the user, rather than assuming it for itself. In this way, every individual can be empowered. Any computer on the network, for example, can become a global broadcasting station.

Only innovation will separate the "big" guy from the "little" guy.

Whether or not churches refuse to go "on-line"—or to move from spectator electronics to interactive multimedia—the gap will still begin to blur between clergy and laity. And worship will still begin to move from the platform to the center of the congregation.

Finally, greater power will form from the "networking" of computers . . . from the synergism of separate sources . . . from teams of intelligence. It will be a win/win victory! For individuals—and teams of individuals—can respond to needs more quickly

. . . more responsively . . . and more flexibly than hidebound institutions.

> "Power that is never surrendered by
> the individual cannot be brokered."[9]

Christian Polity

The new powers are early Christian powers. The old powers are not.

Outside of Scripture, none of the 25,000 documents from early Christianity, mention a "clergyman," "minister," "priest," or "pastor."[10] And "pastor" shows up only once in the New Testament, though we often find references to "elders," "bishops," and "deacons."

In truth, "elder," "bishop," "deacon," "overseer," and "pastor" are interchangeable. Yet, note how Paul directed Titus to appoint elders all over Crete—not pastors! More to the point, an elder was simply a member of the church assembly, not a pious leader with special clerical privileges.[11] Peter—one of the greatest names in Christianity—simply called himself "a fellow elder," and warned other "elders" not to lord it over others.[12]

Luther agreed with all this. So he created the phrase, "the priesthood of all believers"—believing that all Christians were priests to each other as messengers of grace.

Surely, these great men of God would be pleased to see us drop the burdensome past and return, again, to true Christian polity.

> "If you preach, just preach God's
> Message, nothing else; if you help,

just help, don't take over; if you
teach, stick to your teaching; if you
give encouraging guidance, be care-
ful that you don't get bossy; if
you're put in charge, don't manipulate. . . ."[13]

The "Good News"

The new polity means good news for everyone—including
pastors! When clergy mentor . . . and empower the passions of their
laity . . . when they resemble facilitators more than rhetorical
orators . . . when they share an understated, humble, and self-
revealing spirit . . . and when they role model relationships . . . *their
power expands.*

And they get better results. Don E. Miller writes, "Trusting
ministry to lay people and to the Holy Spirit is risky business, but
the payoff is much more diverse, relevant, and responsive program-
ming."[14]

In truth, it is *less* risky, for these new leaders put their eggs
in many baskets, instead of one.

This New Millennium polity is also good news for the laity.
Inspired visions once dormant can break free to act. Because each
person can speak from the center of a networked world . . . each
amplified voice can effect change more than anytime in history.

All one needs is an inspired mind, a loving spirit, a tele-
phone, a modem, and a PC!

Historians have long noted that a creative minority can
reorder society. And scientists—having lost faith in material

reality—now mirror back a world changed by the very act of observing it . . . where the tiniest change in some remote place has system-wide results.

This amazing power means the ecstasy of one soul or the collective creativity of several souls can make waves large enough to change the world.

Small is Beautiful

This upside-down polity typified early Christianity. It never intended to be a top-down faith. It started with individuals . . . then moved to families . . . and finally to neighbors.

After all, salvation comes first to one person. A change of heart derives directly from one-on-one Truth. And its meditation builds strictly personal relationships.

There's nothing institutional about it.

Then—after this personal encounter—it expands to include the family . . . and finally others. In the earliest church, for example, personal bonds formed from small groups meeting in homes. And in the later dispersed church, spiritual kinship formed from shared leadership meeting in synagogues.

From the beginning, it was a "small is beautiful" idea that found endless Scriptural support. The book of Acts, for example, begins with a small band of disciples.[15] Then later letters report a continued shared leadership . . . a "royal priesthood"[16] of *all* believers. Indeed—with proper anointing—anyone could be an apostle, prophet, or evangelist.

Whether they were or not, one thing was certain: Anyone could lead worship:

> When you meet together, *each one* has a hymn, a teaching, a disclosure of special knowledge or information, an utterance in a [strange] tongue, or an interpretation of it.[17]

Throughout Paul's letters, no one escaped one-on-one leadership. Repeatedly he writes, "admonish one another," "edify one another," "prefer one another," "love one another," "receive one another," "greet one another," "serve one another," "forgive one another," "comfort one another". . . .

So when it comes to empowering individuals, the first century church is our model.

Intimate Trends

Strangely enough, the global economy will follow a similar model. As Negroponte puts it, "The digital age is based on a model of you as an individual, not as part of a group."[18]

We're returning to the grassroots!

Mass production, mass distribution, mass education, mass media, and mass entertainment—in their present forms—are becoming things of the past. We find fewer and fewer "faces in the crowd."

Global networks, as well, are becoming the twentieth-century version of the first-century village—sharing, or doing things for "one another." "Unlike the Walkman, a technological revolution that created isolation, the next wave will be all about community, communications, and sharing what we know."[19]

Amazingly, the digital age may even re-empower the family. When television sets become computers (within months), the home will increasingly become the center for work, learning, recreation, fellowship, health care—even shopping and voting. Notice, already the home video market is bigger than the Hollywood movie industry.

We find many of today's churches returning to the first century model. Believers are joining small, intimate fellowships. The majority of churches in this nation have fewer than one hundred members, and as many as 100,000 churches list fewer than thirty-five. Further, most major Christian movements arc focusing on *relational* issues. And, increasingly, the "glitz, trappings, and crutches of present worship are giving way to a more relational, intimate, and interactive worship."[20]

Truly, we see trends toward intimacy.

The "Fear of Man"

Turning the church upside-down releases the pent-up power of grassroots believers. Limits disappear. Walls come down. Individual creativity, interests, decisions, and knowledge interact and create value. Spiritual kinships, bonds, fellowships, and relationships connect and create community.

And the Church benefits.

Downsizing the burdensome infrastructures of top-heavy piety releases resources for global missions. A new agility and a new flexibility allow the Church to grow and change as the world grows and changes. And a new technology and a new paradigm allow the Church to be both large and small in the same instant . . . both global and personal in the same moment.

A relationship to God does not trickle down from the top of an institutional structure. It begins small—with one person. Then it spreads to family, neighbors, and finally to the world.

Yet, many do not see this truth. So there will be increasing conflict between the old Christendom and the new Church . . . between permissible knowledge and forbidden knowledge . . . between the pious powerful of the past and the anointed nobodies of the future.

Why? Because some clergy "fear man" more than God.

> "Personal knowledge is always a
> challenge to accepted opinions and a
> threat to established institutions . . .
> It is no wonder that the church has
> been chary of these claims."[21]

9. CROSSING FORBIDDEN BORDERS

Anyone, Anywhere, Anytime, Anyway

The church of the future must enter previously excluded paths . . . invade priestly restricted areas . . . and cross devoutly forbidden borders.

By tradition, these boundaries separate sacred and secular . . . religious and nonreligious . . . pious and profane . . . clergy and laity . . . church and world . . . familiar and foreign . . . "us" and "them." At first, these polarities defended stability and endurance. But they also refused new ideas, and their opposing choices have scant meaning today.

The new mission requires reaching anyone, anywhere, anytime, anyway. As a result, the twenty-first century spiritual frontier means reaching "different"souls, in "different" places, at "different" times, and in "different" ways.

"There are now literally thousands of teachers and spiritual leaders moving across cultural boundaries."[1] Why not the "established" church? After all, the resources of the church include the Bible, the Holy Spirit, time, space, and believers. The last four are flexible!

Why must there be restrictions?

Very Much in Switzerland

> "We . . . love to set limitations on
> when, where, and how God can
> work. For instance, God can bring
> people to Christ in living rooms and
> at prayer breakfasts, but not in of-
> fices, public housing complexes, or
> bars."[2]

Today's church is a specific community in a specific time
and a specific place. Such dependable visibility will always serve
a purpose. Yet, in this time-zoned, brick and mortar form, the
church lacks the flexibility to respond to the reality of a digital
world.

In the digital world, space changes to cyberspace. Clear
borders between here and there vanish. No longer is there "a place
for everything and everything in its place," writes Marshall
McLuhan. Or, put more painfully perhaps, "You can't go home
again."

Because bits are borderless. Everything gets large and small
at the same time. In fact, this global movement is both chicken and
egg where "Which comes first?" is not even the issue. It is driven
by global skills, for example, yet it also drives local skills.

Already, businesses work at both the local and global level.
Already, partners move beyond old borders. Already, offices
become less and less a place.

It is a global system.

Just notice the phone calls made from cars and planes. Just recall our Internet address works anywhere. Just realize whoever sends us a message has no idea where either we or the message might be.

This omniprescence means, of course, workers are working anywhere. Urban writers and money managers, for example, find it easy—and far more fun—to work in the Caribbean or the South Pacific.

We find examples of on-line communities. "MUDs" and "MOOs" allow surfers from around the world to share the same virtual space. In fact, "MOOs" have become the clubs and coffee houses, the pubs and cafes of the Internet.

Let's face it. Even now, the Internet harbors a virtual "church," for cyberspace serves as a sanctuary—a place of refuge—for restless cyber-nomads.

> "Digital living will include less and less dependence upon being in a specific place at a specific time . . . If I really could look out the electronic window of my living room in Boston and see the Alps, hear the cowbells, and smell the (digital) manure in summer, in a way I am very much in Switzerland."[3]

"In Spirit and Truth"

So Cyberspace churches will function free of time and space. They will be non-territorial . . . non-local. Their on-line communities will be dispersed communities . . . electronic communities . . . virtual communities—imaginary places where those of like faith join together.

This vision of an electronic community does not mean all churches will be "on-line." It does mean, though, all churches will know a new "space." They may look the same, but they will think differently.

And, finally, they will even look differently.

The irrelevance of a worship "place" would not surprise the first century church. Jesus said, "Wherever two or three are gathered . . . I AM in the midst of them."[4] And for emphasis, He told the Samarian woman not to worship God in a *place*, but "in spirit and truth."[5]

It's crucial that churches look beyond the old problems of distance and delivery. For the future is simple: Information, communication, and community were always central to the church, and wherever they happen—"in spirit and truth"—that's the Church!

> "Virtual churches might be just as good as those in the physical world in the sense that they can provide religious experiences."[6]

The Clock Overthrown

Time is shifting as well as space, for the limits of time mean little in the coming age. Digital time resembles more a "present eternity" where the endless reality of the past and the virtual reality of the future flood each moment.

Digital time is also flexible. Networks enable businesses to work anytime. So companies now open 24-hours a day, because they serve all the time zones of the world!

The same immediacy and flexibility already appear in on-line churches. The "Word," for example, is a random access medium, no longer dependent on the hour, or the time required for delivery.

Even off-line or traditional churches will soon find the freedom of this new "time." Increasingly, services will hold ongoing gatherings. Open ended and less agenda driven, worship will flow like a continuous conversation, and "real time" interaction will be the order of the day. Boschman reports there are already churches in Russian with twelve services Sunday. And, in Argentina, some churches meet ten times a day . . . most days of the week.

This should not surprise us. In King David's time, teams of worshipers sang, danced, played music, and prophesied in rotating shifts . . . day and night!

All this is good news. It overthrows the rigid regime of the clock. Let's be honest. We are constantly interrupted or forced into being punctual for things that do not truly merit the demands of promptness. A new definition of time will allow us to glimpse luminous meaning through and beyond the absurdity and monotony of clock time.

As churches envision a digital future, we need to find ways to reach souls anywhere, anytime. Then, in reaching across these frontiers, old borders of space and time will begin to blur.

A Radical Fellowship

The church must also cross cultural cleavages—the borders between "us" and "them." It must transcend its own myopic ways and embrace true diversity. For the digital word will break down ideological walls.

Though the digital revolution—like rock music—appeals to every culture, it still "de-massifies" culture. It thrives on diversity. It honors individuality.

In the past, national and ethnic forces drove the church. Without apologies, missionaries recreated the non-Christian world in their own cultural image. With some, for example, Jesus was unmistakably a white European. So difference was discouraged, sameness encouraged.

Today, though, computer networks call into question our authoritarian assumptions. Increasingly, churches are adapting forms of worship unlike their historical tradition. Recent polls, for example, reveal that two-thirds of the unchurched will accept only a "personal," "noninstitutional" Church experience.[7]

It's clear the church must explore cross-cultural meanings, multicultural expressions, and even counter-cultural idioms. After all, Christianity began as a counter cultural movement—at odds with the prevailing view. Yet, it was also inclusive—embracing everyone. In truth, it was a *radical* fellowship. Paul said that in Christ, "there is neither Jew nor Greek . . . slave nor free . . . male nor female."[8]

And—after 2,000 years—Paul's vision is returning. Global church growth wildly crosses cultural borders and indifferently ignores denominational labels.

"Because of decadence, the Western
way of life is less and less likely to
become the leading model."[9]

Pulling Versus Pushing

Next, leaders must break old communication barriers.

The church continues outdated paradigms of distance
delivery. It still follows old models of "pushed" information. It
still uses the—soon obsolete—one-way, one-to-many media of
books, tapes, TV, and radio. It still oversees the ancient gates of the
Gospel and still micro-manages the story of a "good-old-time
religion."

In short, the Good News is something done "to" us.

In turn, we've become passive spectators . . . careless
listeners . . . naive vessels into which the church simply pours the
Gospel. And often, success depends on marketed manipulation,
complete with excitement and novelty.

But in the digital age, the listener is in charge! He initiates
events. For the computer moves beyond the paradigm of "delivery"
to open interactions . . . dynamic relationships . . . and real-time
responses.

Tapscott calls it "the Age of Networked Intelligence."[10]

After all, the digital medium "dialogues." Its information
flows "two-ways." Broadly defined, the "Net" simply allows all the
world's computers to communicate. Each computer reigns
sovereign yet functions as a peer of others. It chooses its own input,
responds with an opinion, and then says, "tell me more."

Pulling has replaced pushing.

A New Evangelism

The signs of the times reveal this new paradigm.

Already, the Internet nurtures on-line dialogue. One-to-many or many-to-many chats spark excitement in "newsgroups," "usenets," "bulletin boards," and "listserv" lists. Members can address the group as a whole, ask questions, make comments, and learn from others. Both mentors and seekers from around the world can find their own access level.

These dialogues require both "pulling" and "producing." We can reach into the network and check out something the way we do in a library or video store. We can cast about for data, programs, and services. We can explore our interests and find out what we like.

At the same time, we are also "producers." Every traveler on the digital highway becomes a producer when creating and sending messages, sharing a chat room dialogue, changing the end of a movie, or even test driving a virtual car.

This means evangelism will change. In finding the new meaning of neighbors . . . in honoring a new dialogue . . . in respecting autonomous peers, the old paradigm of mass manipulation will fail.

If the church could only see that.

"Discovery . . . this is Mission Control"

Again, we're speaking of more than an on-line church, for the present church—on-line or off-line—will also change. In many ways, it will return to the oral medium of the first century church. It will grow more "interactive," for example.

After all, one trait that most separates Christianity from Eastern religions is "interaction"—a bedrock belief that embraces both passive receiving and active responding.

Early Hebrew study, for example, loved the interplay between text and comment . . . between the "Word" and personal insight. This was true of all the Talmudic commentaries. It was an "active/passive" meditation. Or as Richard of Saint-Victor wrote, "Meditation investigates; contemplation wonders."

First century worship embraced the same interactivity. In fact, each worshiper played a role in the outcome of worship. In other words, worship was not something done "to" or "for" the believers. It was done "by" the believers.

Except for Jesus and Peter talking to the crowds, the oral medium of early Christianity did not "broadcast" to the masses. Mostly, it shared a *rhema* word—a specific message to a specific person at a specific time . . . and requiring a specific response.

Rex Miller has a great metaphor for the return of the first century church:

> The whole congregation will have a new focus on the "service," similar to the way a flight control room participates in the launching and bringing back of the space shuttle. The crew is in space, and

we are in the control room. And all of it is held
together by technology.

Computers on Camels

This means digital bits must become increasingly "user-
friendly." To understand the message right, we must get the
language right. The syntax must satisfy a particular people, a
particular culture. So the church must enable real people to speak
of real issues . . . in real time . . . in real language.

The early church provides the example. Its symbols—though foreign today—emerged from secular life. Its
Scripture—though elegant today—leaped from street language. So
it's time for our theology to move from head to heart . . . from ivory
tower to control tower . . . from theory to practice. Or in the words
of Sally Morgenthaler,

> It would hardly be responsible to prescribe irrele-
> vance in an age when fewer than three in ten people
> consider the church to be relevant! If anything, we
> need to increase our ability to speak in the vernacu-
> lar of our time.[11]

This means the church's New Millennium mission must
provide "user-friendly" access to every global citizen. Fortunately,
computers will continue to increase in availability and decrease in
price. Soon—like the ubiquitous Walkman—computers will ride
the camels of the Sahara. Nevertheless, the church must ensure no
one is left out.

> "We are entering an era when ex-
> pression can be more participatory
> and alive."[12]

Hard Fun

Finally, the church must break generational barriers. For "the dominant forces (on the Internet) are not social or racial or economic, but generational. The have's and the have-not's are *now* the young and the old . . . (It is) the *real* cultural divide."[13]

This is the first generation to be born into homes with computers. More important, this is the first generation to "play" with computers. In fact, today's children have a passion for the hard fun of information-rich games. And the advanced toys they now play with and the skillful tools they will someday work with are the same.

"It is almost genetic in its nature, in that each generation will become more digital than the preceding one."[14]

Even today, the average age of an Internet user is twenty-one and declining,[15] and ferocious competition forces these career youth to innovate constantly.

Clearly, the young are in charge.

In the past, the church catered to the young simply to replace aging believers. Simply to survive! But today, calling the young the "next generation" will prove a tragic error. They are the "now generation," and the sooner we see this the better.

"Let us trust the young . . . They
have had the advantage of growing
up with these new developments,
and it will be their duty to employ
these new instruments for a wider
and more intense dialogue among all
the diverse races and classes who
share this 'shrinking globe'."

Pope John Paul II[16]

IV. THE PROPHETIC

10. NEEDING A NEW "WORD"

Searching for Miracles

Storytelling changes. At first, the sages spoke their stories. Then they embalmed them in text. Today, of course, we broadcast them with pictures. And tomorrow . . . ?

Already tomorrow's words move too fast to guarantee their future out of a much slower past. Already new stories emerge in forms totally unknown by earlier norms. And already digital thoughts fly terribly apace beyond known time and space.

The "end of modernity"—it's often called—even questions our privileged point of view . . . our single story . . . our harmonized history.[1] Today, for example, the Christian voice is only one among many. Yes, we can reach the whole world, but so can every other voice . . . every other faith . . . every other belief.

Nothing stops them.

Because in cyberspace, the difference between "here" and "there" begins to blur. The difference between "them" and "us" ceases to exist. And—to be expected the difference between orthodoxy and heresy turns trivial.

How can we claim the ultimate "Word" when the future refuses such a privilege?

It's not enough for the church to embrace modern skills . . . it's not enough to tell better stories . . . it's not even enough to speak the latest lingo. Something miraculously different is required.

Religious "Words"?

Yes, the church trusts God's Word. But too often, it also trusts "religious words"—the form and routine of liturgies and litanies. So clergy and congregations "do doctrines" . . . "carry out creeds" . . . sequence ceremonies in certain ways.

These are the proper "words" . . . the fixed prayers and rituals legislated by the professionally pious. After all, "liturgy" demands "a *prescribed* form of religious service." But these carefully crafted confessions often emerge from theological posturing: "We do it right here . . . They do it wrong over there."

The histories of these liturgies stack one tradition on another, each immutable . . . each "divinely instituted." Yet, like the layers of an onion, we must peel off each added dogma to get back to where the Church began. But cautious clerics are not into onion peeling, so they force obsolete styles onto a secular society. "We've asked the unchurched to go through a painful, cultural circumcision in order to become a Christian."[2]

Then, the best of our intended "words" become "the perfection of empty precision . . . soulless and insensate, lethal, immaculate in its vanity."[3]

Greek "Words"?

Many believers also abide by "logical" words . . . "credible" words . . . "reliable" words . . . 'schooled" words. And—for centuries—these words have been those officially ordained by the ancient Greeks.

In truth, Western Civilization is more Greek than Christian!

The Greek legacy of theology, philosophy, and science has often replaced Scripture as the final "Word"... especially after the invention of the printing press. With the printed word, books *about* Scripture began to spread... then books about books... interpreters answering interpreters... texts mimicking texts... in a long and dreary intellectual history.

And somewhere on this journey, the facts of faith replaced the experience of faith... objective truth replaced subjective truth... and reasoning replaced revelation.

Most denominational believers, for example, find their "Word" through knowledge—that is, through rational argument, religious apology, critical reasoning, and skillful judgment... a kind of divine philosophy. Descarte—the father of modern philosophy—said, "I think, therefore I am." Further, "True knowledge comes only from reason."

But Carl Jung called Descarte's faithful descendants "reason-mongers."

The ancient Greeks also gave birth to modern science. So today, spiritual truth must stand the test of objective facts, observable proof, and reliable statistics. After all, the Greek word for truth (*aletheia*) means "reality." This reality, of course, requires divorcing fact from feeling, mind from body, and intellect from intuition. Both liberals and fundamentalists agree with these commands, for "God must be reduced, after all, to workable ideas."

This "credible" word—this literal word—is especially at home on the printed page, and its rhetorical cousin—the skilled word—empowers preachers. "The preacher did a good job," critical observers say when they are persuaded with the rhetoric of effective language and logical argument. So in these churches . . . worship and the sermon are the same.

The Final Tombstone

But the Greeks are finished—then and now! Postmodern scholars are "highly suspicious of any interpretation of reality that attributes stability, solidity and permanent validity to the worlds of our discourse."[4] In other words, today's words are just words. Or, more ominously, some scholars believe our words are mere "constructs of false consciousness imposed by those in power."[5]

Even the "words" of science have changed. The rational, mechanical past has given way to a dynamic, expanding future. And the latest physics moves more in a cosmos of music than in the realm of math. In fact, yesterday's reality melts quickly into myth.

But the digital age will place the final tombstone over our deceased Greek legacy. "On the computer, the text . . . takes on a plasticity like that of clay to the potter. It can be molded and remolded. It can be twisted, reordered, restored. The meaning of a text, consequently, is as malleable as the text itself."[6]

In short, the "authority" of the text disappears.

Further, digital words have a short shelf-life. As soon as they confront us, still newer words rapidly replace them. And within their ephemeral life, the interplay of context and consensus constantly reorganizes knowledge. Or, often, this knowledge serves as a modern, stripped down "technojargon for computer hackers and Coca-Cola salesmen of a global society."[7]

This disappearing Greek legacy presents no great loss, for Greek words—according to Paul—never revealed spiritual wisdom in the first place. Paul said God's Word is not "the word of [mere] men." Paul's "treasures of wisdom," for example, were neither "intelligence," "a critical faculty," nor "understanding."[8] For the Kingdom of God, he said, stands on "power"—"not talk." So he gave his message without "lofty words of eloquence or human philosophy and wisdom." He did not stoop to mere "(enticing and plausible) words."[9]

Let's face it, the basic life questions of ancient Greece remain unanswered even today. For finally, changes of the heart sway us—not rational arguments alone.

> "Far too many ministers . . . devote
> hours and hours to the preparation of
> sermons, blissfully unaware that the
> sermon as we know it is dead."[10]

Up-to-date "Words"?

Then, many well-intentioned leaders pursue "up-to-date" words. And, true enough, declaring the gospel with the latest lingo sounds smart . . . but it begs the question. For "new wine skins" are not enough, Jesus implied. We must also have "new wine."[11]

New wine skins alone—just the packaging itself—means relevance without depth . . . the secular without the sacred . . . the flesh without the faith. In short, the content becomes negotiable! *The Message Bible* puts it this way: "Don't reduce holy mysteries to slogans. In trying to be relevant, you're only being cute and inviting sacrilege."[12] Again, "We don't take God's Word, water it down, and then take it to the streets to sell it cheap."[13]

Nevertheless, market-driven churches are alive, though not too well. They begin by asking a skeptical secular society what it wants the church to be like. Then they take these stylish trends and package them for the flesh among their faithful. In short, these managers of the sacred almost "rig" worship. And, of course, their churches end up not only "in the world," but "of the world."

Perhaps we can say, "The end justifies the means." But problems appear when we lift up the means as an end in itself. Instead of "The Word becoming flesh," "The flesh becomes 'Word'."

Take "contemporary Christian" music as example. No doubt, it speaks the voice of our time. No doubt, it proves its power on a global scale. But if we remove all the religious words, often only secular sounds remain. And these sounds—by themselves—only celebrate who we are . . . not who God is. We simply look at ourselves in the mirror.

Strangely enough, the so-called "new" in these faddish trends is not really new. There's a difference, after all, between "trends" and "transformations." Congregations, for example, easily weary of mere novelty, and when they do, they slip into empty ritual with the "new" as with the old.

> "Don't fool yourself. Don't think
> that you can be wise merely by being
> up-to-date with the times . . . (God)
> exposes the chicanery of the chic.
> The Master sees through the smoke
> screens of the know-it-alls."[14]

Ancient "Words"?

But some leaders suspect cheap trends. These "words" of the future frighten them. So they react to change . . . they wistfully search the distant past and longingly restore its antiquities. Their nostalgia, for example, recently rocketed a monastery recording to the top of the pop charts.

Obviously, we should plumb the depths of the early church. We should search the lost pages of its history. We should make this our worthy cause!

But the Hebrew Christians are not our saviors! Their cultural "words" are not *the* Word. Just because the gospel unfolded in a particular culture does not mean that culture itself is sacred. If it were, then all men should be circumcised, and all the angry righteous should tear their clothes.

Yet, a wistful desire for the past crosses ever so easily a forbidden line. It sets apart the past as a sacrament itself. It turns old metaphors into objects of innate awe and mystical power. Even in ancient times, Jeremiah warned that trust in outward forms of religion without inward bonds to the Lord was deceptive. He called, instead, for new "Words written on the heart."[15]

> "If you only love God enough, you may safely follow all your inclinations."
>
> Saint Augustine

New Age "Words"?

While denomination churches still trust in Greek "words" or ancient "words," and post-denomination churches still trust in popular "words," most secular leaders ignore both groups. Instead, they prefer New Age "words." These cutting-edge pioneers embrace the prevalent "new world" view: a personal, nonrational, anything-goes, global mysticism.

John wrote, "In the beginning was the Word," and he insisted this Word still reigns. But John didn't know today's New Agers. For they know only a slippery, "maybe" truth—relative and pragmatic.

"It just depends," they say.

With the New Ager, truth exists only with their approval . . . only if it seems right at the moment . . . only if it fits their context.

Then . . . they justify it.

No doubt, the frontiers of science open to relative realities beyond our wildest dreams. But to apply these revelations to the lying lives of imperfect souls . . . to all the little games we play . . . to our ongoing war with selfishness . . . only distorts our already tenuous hold on Truth.

For then, truth becomes opinion . . . faith becomes skepticism . . . fact becomes fancy . . . liberation becomes license. And the digital age only exaggerates this corruption. Soon, the world will manipulate a "virtual" truth . . . it will "cut and paste" a New Age "Word" . . . and it will assemble a collage of beliefs. And it will do it all within the questionable consensus of a "global consciousness."

> "Artificial intelligence, artificial life,
> virtual reality are involved in . . . a

complete deconstruction of the
whole value system."

William Irwin Thompson[16]

————— ••••••• —————

So neither religious "words," Greek "words," up-to-date
"words," ancient "words," nor New Age "words" can carry us into
the New Millennium. Nor can their style, tradition, or doctrine
manipulate God's presence.

In the debate between these "words," everyone loses, for
they are all humanly chosen ends—"words" with a small "w."
Worship is first and foremost an encounter with God. Only
secondarily has it anything to do with what we "do."

Clearly, we need something different.

Almost three thousand years ago, Hosea explained the
difference—the rules for this Divine encounter . . . the language of
a another Word. It worked then, and it will prove a requisite in the
New Millennium. In the next chapter, we'll explore this old—yet
"new"—Word.

11. REDISCOVERING *DAMAH*

From Monologue to Dialogue

Changing realities and changing lifestyles require a changing church. But the surface measures of *self*-reform—*our* reform —cannot move the hand of God . . . no matter how hard we try. Worship is not a higher horizon of pious performance. Nor is it a sharpened summons of God's presence. Let's face it: No ritual has power in itself. For a symbol—Tillich points out—"points only out of the power to which it points."

What does this mean?

It means worship is a dialogue—not a monologue . . . an anointing—not a procedure . . . an inspiration—not an invention. It means worship claims its own time and place . . . its own form and fashion . . . its own familiarity or unfamiliarity. And it means worship moves just as easily outside of religion as within religion . . . outside of tradition as within tradition . . . outside of piety as within piety.

Put simply, worship manifests when Spirit takes on body and body takes on Spirit. And this dialogue can occur anytime . . . anywhere . . . anyway.

For years we sang *about* God, for example. Our hymns and songs exclaimed to each other the wonderful things God has done. More recently, we discovered singing *to* God. The texts of songs, in other words, shifted from third person to second person. Now it's time to let God sing too!

The future promises such a dialogue.

Dialogue and Damah

But how?

The prophet Hosea already told us. Yet, we've missed it!

Hosea described three ways God speaks to the faithful: (1) through "prophets" (inspired believers), (2) through "visions" (direct intuitive revelations), and (3) through *damah* in the Hebrew—meaning "comparisons of likeness."[1]   Today, these intuitive comparisons of inspired believers should be called "prophetic metaphors."

Hosea's *damah* and "prophetic metaphor," in other words, mean the same in these chapters.

Defining Hosea's prophecy further, a prophet is an inspired believer who shares a vision with others. A vision is an intuitive revelation that speaks more to the heart than to the mind. And *damah* is the "form"—the words, music, images, and the like—that prophets bring to their vision.

In other words, without *damah*, there is no form . . . no shared vision . . . and, finally, no worship. *Damah*, then, becomes the essential dialogue of worship—a dialogue between believers and their God. This fact becomes evermore crucial, for we will discover that the digital age returns us to the age of *damah*.

But first, let's recall the words of inspired biblical writers. They were creators of comparison and contrast . . . artists of analogy and affinity . . . virtuosos of similarity and similitude. In short, they spoke the language of prophetic metaphor.

Even from the beginning, "God said, Let Us . . . make
mankind in Our image, after Our *likeness*."[2] And later, Ezekiel—
among many—wrote, "The Lord came to me, saying . . . utter a
parable."[3] So Ezekiel uttered a "likeness"[4] . . . a resemblance . . .
a comparison of the unfamiliar with the familiar, of the real with the
unreal.

Jesus resumed the same sacred similitudes when He said,
"With what can we *compare* the kingdom of God, or what *parable*
(*damah*) shall we use to illustrate and explain it?" And four verses
later, Mark said Jesus "did not tell them *anything* without a
parable."[5] In fact, parables and miracles of parables confirmed His
entire ministry. And finally, His very death and resurrection, Paul
said, were metaphors of our own death and life in this lifetime.[6]

In a word, Jesus was the ultimate metaphor!

Later, Paul echoed, again, Hosea's truth: The "Eye hath not
seen, nor ear heard . . . the things which God hath prepared." "But
God hath revealed them unto us by . . . *comparing* spiritual things
with spiritual."[7] And so it goes . . . one sacred metaphor after
another . . . throughout the entire Bible. Clearly, God intended to
speak to us through *damah* . . . through prophetic metaphor.

Defining Damah

But this metaphor is not a literary metaphor . . . not a mere
figure of speech . . . not a mental trick. For years, scholars threw all
metaphors into a common basket of colorful idioms. But now they
know another metaphor that has nothing to do with such clever
devices. Now they know a metaphor that has the power to point
beyond our known world . . . beyond us . . . and beyond the
metaphor itself.[8]

Neither is this metaphor a tool of the logical or natural mind. It is "not written with ink," Paul said, "but with the Spirit of the living God . . . (on) human hearts."[9] When Paul wrote, for example, "Faith comes by hearing, and hearing by the Word of God," he was talking about the *rhema* Word—a Word that speaks first to the heart.[10]

This means *damah*—or prophetic metaphor—requires emotion. Of their own volition, Hosea's words quicken the scarlet memories of sin and the pure joy of snow. But they quicken a "knowing" emotion, a spiritual emotion—not the fickle, pseudo-pious emotion of the natural soul. For *damah* is an "otherworldly" language that speaks with "otherworldly" emotion. The term "metaphor," for example, comes from *metaphora* in the Greek, meaning "to carry across." And, in this case, our spiritual feelings translate meaning from one realm to another.

This is the very nature of worship! By means of signs perceived by the senses, our sensations are signified. Even secular experts confirm this intuitive language. Frank Barron reports, "Intuition depends . . . on (both) feelings and metaphor."[11] And the theologian Robert Webber calls the "signs and symbols" of our worship, "presence carriers."[12]

A Perfect Model

But there's more to *damah* than sacred emotion. *Damah* was also the "art" of the ancient Hebrews. And—as Hosea explained —Hebrew prophets were also artists.

The majority of the prophetic books in the Bible, for example, are lyric oracles or poetic songs. In fact, artistic skills were a prophetic necessity. When Jehoshaphat asked Elisha to prophesy, he said, "First bring me a musician."[13] When David appointed prophets, he demanded musicians (288 of them!).[14] Indeed, prophets and artists were so closely connected Ezekiel complained when his listeners thought of him as "just another performer."[15]

And the prophets didn't limit themselves to music. Sometimes they acted out their anointing. Hosea, for example, said God's metaphors were "acted out by prophets."[16] In truth, Jeremiah, Ezekiel, and Hosea all had ministries of drama.[17]

Only recently we discovered that the rules for *damah*—the rules for a prophetic metaphor—represent the very structure of art . . . a perfect model of art . . . then and now.[18] The rediscovery of this ancient truth promises incredible revelations. If we understand the laws of this metaphor, we will finally understand the laws of all the arts . . . the awesome power of worship . . . and the postmodern language of the digital age.

We must be cautious, however. This ancient *damah* contained broader understandings of art and worship than the ones we hold today. Today, for example, we separate art into autonomous artistic domains—music, poetry, visual art, drama, and dance. Not so the Hebrews, where even the simple act of breaking bread released cosmic power.

And today, we mistakenly divide worship into acceptably holy moments—separating the sacraments from the superfluous . . . the significant from the insignificant . . . the pious from the profane . . . the pretty from the ugly . . . the dignified from undignified . . . the "high mass" from the "low mass" . . . and all the other carry overs from the disreputable Gnostics and the secular Greeks.

Damah, on the other hand, is the language of life—ordinary . . . common. And, like a hall of mirrors, it speaks throughout worship in endless multiples of form, time, and place. That's why this historical moment is truly significant. For the multimedia, multisensory world of the digital age will prove a perfect haven for powerful prophetic metaphors. And the intense, innovative interaction of this new environment will promise a perfect platform for empowered prophetic voices.

From Ideas to Images

We should jump at this chance.

But our rational reasons and sound-bite senses adjust poorly to the hidden references of prophetic metaphor: "Why not tell it the way it is?" "Why all this artifice in the first place?" Even the disciples were relieved when Jesus finally stopped His riddles: "Ah, now You are speaking plainly to us and not in parables."[19]

Why indeed? Because our natural eyes and natural mind are "incapable," Paul says, "of knowing (God)!"[20] But when we move from flesh to spirit, our knowing shifts from ideas to images . . . from abstract thought to living drama . . . from simply thinking to prophetic projection. That's the reason theologian H. A. Williams insists, "We can know God 'absolutely' only in analogy and through metaphor."

Even salvation, Jonathan Edwards wrote, requires a sensibility to the images of beauty. He would agree with the psalmist: "*Taste* and *see* that the Lord is good."[21]

But, finally, we must admit our very lives journey with metaphor. Take the word "journey," as example. Often we say, "It's been a long bumpy road" . . . "but now I'm marching to a different drummer" . . . "I took the path less taken" . . . "and it'll be smooth sailing from here on". . . .

In short, life is a journey, and the journey is a metaphor.

————— ••••◉•••• —————

Styles and traditions of worship will come and go, but *damah* will always remain. Nothing could be more basic . . . nothing could least deserve blindness . . . and nothing could prevent its digital version. So let us begin our understanding of a prophetic metaphor—the dynamics, the skills, the insights. . . .

12. THE DYNAMICS OF *DAMAH*

"The flesh made word"

God wills to approach and be approached. And, through His prophets, He clearly shows how this happens. It happens through *damah*—or what we call prophetic metaphor. And this metaphor—this divine communion—stands as an imperative in the New Millennium.

Three simple components form a prophetic metaphor: (1) the "known," (2) the "unknown," and (3) the "transcendent." Sacred power requires all three.

When Isaiah said, "Though your sins be as scarlet, they shall be white as snow,"[1] the words, "scarlet," "white," and "snow"—on their own—had nothing to do with sin. In the rational world, they made no sense. Yet, the prophet compared these known words to their unknown reference to sin. He held the tension between what is and what is not. He drew a possible likeness from the supposedly alike—though in reality, the unalike.

And the results were transcendent! Sin and grace became unlikely illuminated in the light of scarlet stains and spotless snow.

By analogy, these tensions between the "known" and the "unknown" appear also in the arts. They appear in any art form and on several levels at once! This should not surprise us. We've already learned that a prophetic metaphor is a miniature work of art.[2] Indeed, it represents the very structure of art . . . a perfect model of art! At the simplest level, for example, pigments of paint are mere matter and have no known link to the visions in a painting. Pieces of stone are only minerals and refuse affinity with the faces in a statue. And vibrations of sound are simply molecules and know nothing of the feelings in a song.

We know that paint, stone, and sound are common facts, but in the *damah* of art, they move us into another world. And, though unsaid, we intuitively marvel, "What do these natural facts have to do with these numinous feelings?"

The same dynamics—the "known," the "unknown," and the "transcendent"—occur also in worship . . . or whenever and wherever "the Word becomes flesh."

The "Known"

There are good reasons for the "known" in a prophetic metaphor. First, truth speaks through known symbols. After all, God deigned to take on flesh, including common sense senses. They are relevant! And, today, this relevance becomes evermore compelling; for life moves with increasing speed, and we have to hang onto something.

That something is a common language—the words in which we shop and talk. That something is our tradition—our way of thinking, our established notions. And, finally, that something is the sight and sound, the taste and touch, the aroma and rhythm of the familiar and friendly. In short, we hold dear those things that rank second only to our face and name. And, though church doctrines seem our very own, true familiarities are usually not "religious."

Even so, the prophetic metaphors of worship cannot exist without the "known." When the expected . . . the routine . . . and the credible seem absent, the "unknown" becomes confused chaos.

Or, when the ordinary . . . the obvious . . . and the orderly appear missing, the "unknown" can turn to terror.

So the "known" in a prophetic metaphor must be known! We must know snow, for example, before we can know Isaiah's "snow." Especially in a global world. Otherwise, the "known" in one culture will be "unknown" in another . . . the code language in one institution will sound strange in another . . . the trendy style of one congregation will appear alien in another.

The "Unknown"

Interrupting the "known" in a prophetic metaphor . . . trespassing its common relevance, marches the bold "unknown." And with good reason. The "unknown" is the only thing that dismantles a worn-out past . . . plants the seeds of new possibilities . . . and permits the journey of pristine revelation.

In the beginning, of course, the "unknown" simply differs from the "known." Isaiah's "snow," for example, is a far cry from "sin." With an impertinent intrusion, the "unknown" shows how it deviates from—even disagrees with—the "known." It fearlessly flaunts anything contradictory . . . out of order . . . unrelated. It risks the total destruction of the expected . . . the broken rules of the requisite . . . and the dismantling of the day-to-day.

And—like the "known"—the prophetic metaphors of worship are impossible without the "unknown." When unknown play and parody never appear, the "known" seems stale, sickenly routine. When a carnival-like violation of the ordinary never occurs, the "known" turns tedius, even tiresome.

So it's important that Isaiah's "snow" disagrees totally with "sin" and "grace." It's necessary that his comparison sounds incredible. And it's required that he proclaims this contradiction with boldness.

A Reciprocal Relation

But the real secret of *damah* is neither the "known" nor the "unknown." It is the tension between them . . . the suspense in their reciprocal relation . . . the risk in their rapport.

It's what happens when we put the two together.

Comparing things that cannot be compared produces the necessary absurdity, nonsense, enigma, or paradox in a metaphor. That's the reason the *Apocrypha* calls *damah* "subtle," "hidden," and "obscure."[3] Yet, within this obscurity, we notice something happening . . . we feel a faint inward movement . . . we sense a divine seduction.

This seduction flows through the unity of depth and relevance . . . inward power and outward form . . . freedom and order. It creates worship that's of another world, yet in this world . . . open to mystery, yet safe and familiar . . . not so familiar as to be mundane, yet not so unfamiliar as to be irrelevant.

Still, prophetic metaphors are not always attractive . . . they are not always comfortably "religious." For they can declare both fascinating mystery and terrifying power. They can paint both unbearable ugliness and overpowering beauty. They can reflect both worldly tragedy and otherworldly triumph

All at the same time!

Yet, this amazing energy—this vivifying principle—comes not from the metaphor itself. It "comes from elsewhere," Paul

Recoeur reports. Or, again in the words of Tillich, "It points out of the power to which it points." So the tension between the "known" and the "unknown" merely represents . . . responds . . . or role-plays. The suspense in their differences looks "to things that are unseen" and gives "substance" to their vision.[4]

So New Millennium church leaders will resemble spear fishermen who throw their spears in places different from the fish, knowing that the original image refracts in the water.

Readers, however, may appreciate this confession: Though the dynamics of *damah* appear simple on the surface, they are complex in their depth. That's because several levels of tension, suspense, and risk occur at the same time: between the "known" and the "unknown," between the metaphor and the power to which it points, between this world and another world, and often, between several metaphors at once.

After all, the "Word" both reveals and conceals.[5]

The same blurring between present signs and absent sources appears in the "virtual reality" of the digital age. Something "virtual" "exists in essence or effect though not in actual fact." Yet, it is essentially the same as the reality it represents.[6]

Finally, however, whether in church or out of church . . . whether in present reality or virtual reality, pure revelation comes only to a "pure heart."[7]

A Virtual Skyscraper

Let's look further . . . let's make music our example:

Artists always wonder how a mere twelve notes in the musical scale can create such endless variety? Now we know. Music births from many tensions between the "known" and the "unknown"—metaphors on top of metaphors . . . a virtual heavenly hierarchy. And these metaphors stretch credibility on several levels at once.

First, there's the basic tension between sound and music. Natural sound is an everyday part of life. It's known. But when formed into music, it no longer qualifies as common sense. It leaves the realm of reality. If a newscaster, for example, suddenly sings the news—as in an opera—we would feel ashamed . . . even horrified!

Yet, this nonsense occurs constantly in music. So our ruined reason reaches for intuitive answers.

Or, consider these metaphors: We take our sense of hearing for granted. It's known. And common sense separates it from other senses. Yet, in music, we also *feel* "warm" tones. Or, we *see* "bright" voices. So again, we find tensions between the "known" and the "unknown"—between merely hearing music and "feeling" it.

But the story of our lost logic continues. . . .

Listen to musicians talk. Their words describe the "movement" of music—how it steps, leaps, shifts, runs, marches, drives, relaxes. . . .   Yet, music can't "move"! Pitches may change—higher, lower, faster, slower, louder, softer—but they can't move! So we confront, again, known "changes," but unknown "movement."

There's also a time warp in music. Music moves in its own "time"—that is, the *experience* of time . . . not clock time. Its tempo paces faster or slower. Its length swells or shrinks. It even moves beyond time! Yet, music cannot alter the known interval of a minute or the common span of an hour.

Then music also sets a mood. And we routinely accept it. We run both shopping malls and dairy farms with it! But the paradox of opposing moods—like struggle and celebration in the same song or even the same moment!—creates an inner tension that drives us toward Spirit. Still, we usually forget that it's the tension *between* moods—not one "milking" mood—that brings the transcendence.

Finally, the elements of music—melody, harmony, rhythm, texture, timbre, and form—all interact. The "known" and "unknown" play not only between each element, but within each element as well. Rhythm, for example, contains a common "beat"—a clock-like, perfunctory pulse that resembles our boring breathing. But breaking this beat with unknown rhythms . . . with surprising punctuations . . . brings breathless wonder.

The same wonder occurs when melody goes against its own direction . . . when harmony goes against its own tonality. . . .

We find, in fact, endless metaphors in music. Other examples include the tensions between past traditions and modern transitions . . . between the events of music and the music itself . . . between the medium of music and other artistic forms. . . .

And so it goes . . . on and on. A virtual skyscraper . . . one metaphoric story on top of the other.

The Church Alive

The church is never more alive than when knowing this . . . when knowing the dynamics of prophetic metaphor. King David combined, at the height of Hebrew worship, both known rules and unknown spontaneity. His skilled musicians, for example, doubled as inspired prophets.[8] Jesus taught with the street language of the day, yet stunned His listeners with hidden content. Even His plainspoken disciples struggled with His cryptic messages.[9] And Paul exhorted his believers with the unlikely pairing of both common sense mind and nonsense spirit. He prayed and sang with both intelligence and intuition.[10]

And this paradox continued. Later Christians retained their known Jewish traditions, yet blatantly proclaimed that their bodies replaced the temple and their souls its priests.[11] They kept, as well, the ancient custom of religious sacrifice. Only now, Christ was the sacrificial lamb!

Christianity, in fact, birthed from placing the routine "known" side by side with the radically "unknown."

Then through the dark ages of the unknown Latin mass, the one thing that kept the Church alive, were the sensory experiences of known music, bells, gestures, processions. . . . While in Eastern Europe, the Orthodox Church survived by the powerful tension between a distant, unknowable God and a personal, knowable God—One "who *nevertheless* dwells among us."[12]

The Reformation continued, at first, with cryptic Catholic ceremonies, while Martin Luther merely added familiar favorites—such as barroom ballads! Soon, however, prophetic metaphors exploded into countless church renewals. The Puritans stressed head knowledge of the Word, yet listened equally with their heart.[13] The Quakers practiced great personal restraint, yet spoke under the compulsion of the Holy Spirit. They also expected a high degree of biblical literacy, yet bowed to corporate mysticism.[14]

Today, a second reformation revolves around the Black Church. Its Pentecostal, charismatic versions have touched every believer on every continent and will continue reshaping religion in the twenty-first century.

Why?

Again, the ageless components of *damah* come into play . . . the deep tensions between the "known" and the "unknown" harbor transcendence. African-Americans celebrate joy, for example, with the same music in which they grieved during slavery. And though their music remains a spirit-moved improvisation, it still bows to unspoken aesthetic bounds.

And black preachers boldly break the white disciplines of Greek rhetoric with inspired images, lusty narratives, striding cadences, and empowered emotions. In short, they blend the sacred and the secular . . . the excellent and the earthy . . . the eternal and the timely.

This juxtaposition of the "known" and the "unknown" is the Church alive!

The "Transcendent"

. . . but only if the "transcendence" in its metaphor is alive.

Notice.

First, we sensed the worldly reality of known images —sounds and sights, touches and tastes, statements and styles. . . . Next we encountered contradictions to these realities . . . the unknown tensions between conflicting images. Then we met a figurative or symbolic level . . . the enigmatic interface between these unrelated ideas. Suddenly, strange notions like "terrible beauty" or "furious calm" stretched credibility and demanded deciphering.

In these moments, we can only intuit the sense . . . the gist . . . the tenor of their meaning. And—if they hold prophetic metaphors—their tenor will transcend both self and society.

That's the goal, after all, of worship!

This transcendence begins with a spiritual "knowing" that is evoked or felt aesthetically—the same way we experience beauty. We hear music, for example, with our ear, but we sense its meaning with an "inner" ear. Metaphor, in other words, plays between the ear and the "inner ear" . . . between "sense" and "non-sense."

This is the language of spirit, for whatever "is born of the Spirit is spirit."[15] This is the language of unspokenness, for "The Kingdom of God . . . is based on not talk but power."[16] And this is the language of emotion, for without feelings, a prophetic metaphor cannot exist.

Paul Valery also called it "a language within a language." And Hans Urs von Balthasar called it the language of beauty, for "divine revelation has an intrinsically aesthetic character . . . in the form it takes and in the response it evokes." Finally, it is the language of personal drama, for it appeals directly and intensely to the heart.

In Saint Paul's wisdom, these "holy emotions" prove the "power of God" operates in us.[17]

Then, something further happens. Sooner or later, the mind and heart bridge their separation. The divine season illuminates blind reason. And we believe the bond between what we feel and something real "out there." We comprehend a coherence . . . a harmony . . . a unity among interconnected things.

In short, we finally "make sense" of our senses.

And the change in perception changes the perceiver. It is a transformation of the heart . . . not mere revisions of opinion. It is a new relation to God . . . not new beliefs about God. For "The old . . . has passed away. Behold, the fresh and new has come!"[18]

> "And it came to pass, as he sat at meat with them, he took bread, and blessed it, and brake, and gave to them. *And their eyes were opened and they knew him*."[19]

What it's Not

Perhaps it's easier, though, to grasp what *damah* is not. And—topping the list—it is not a literal metaphor or a mere figure of speech.

In short, "The medium is *not* the message." With due respect to Marshall McLuhan, literal and prophetic metaphors differ. While literal metaphors are the message, prophetic metaphors are only the messengers . . . the mediums of exchange. Prophetic metaphors, in other words, are neither material nor immaterial . . . neither matter nor spirit . . . but bridges between these two realms.

Truth is realized through them, but not in them.

Anything prophetic is freed of its natural tendency. So a transcendent metaphor points beyond us . . . beyond even the metaphor itself. When the psalmist sang, "The Lord is my Rock, my Fortress,"[20] he was neither singing about "religious rock" nor grooving to a Hebrew "rock" concert. The psalmist and the psalm pointed beyond themselves.

In other words, *damah* is not something we invent . . . a clever catharsis of pent-up passions. For "No prophecy ever originated because some man willed it." "It never came by human impulse." Biblical prophets, in fact, often puzzled over what they proclaimed. And even Peter complained that Paul wrote things hard to explain![21]

That's why Walt Whitman wrote that "music" is "nearer and farther" than either the music or the musicians. That's why Saint Augustine said, "We see one thing but understand something else." And that's why a prophetic metaphor doesn't have to be "religious" in order to be religious!

Obviously, then, the message of this metaphor is not something previously known . . . not something expected . . . not the past warmed over . . . not a regrouping of former insights. And for these reasons, its Truth cannot be paraphrased or literally restated in other forms.

So in this prophetic environment, the familiar becomes strange, and the strange becomes familiar!

Fools Gold

Yet, in the midst of valued things, we imitate valued things. We simulate silver and gold, for example, more than iron and copper. It's no surprise, then, we pass off contrived transcendence as the real thing. So our list of "what *damah* is not" continues:

A prophetic metaphor is not an intellectual skill or a philosopher's trick. It is not, for example, Hegel's "dialectic reasoning." For Hegel's "dialectics" and Hosea's *damah* differ. Hegel's method admittedly begins with a tension between two opposing thoughts. But he resolves the tension with a third thought that simply combines the best of both points of view. In other words, Hegel merely creates a new idea out of old concepts. But in Hosea's *damah*, someone else is the Creator—the "new" is *totally* new, and we discover we are merely the discoverers.

Here is another imitation:

Surrealism. This faddish art warps the metaphoric mirror. It does stress intuitive imagery—including chance effects and unexpected comparisons. But its images are irrational, not trans-rational . . . passive, not prophetic . . . permissive, not promising. In fact, surrealism seeks anything weird, unreal, distorted, twisted . . . even demonic. In short, it only succeeds in bringing the debris of sick souls to the surface.

Or, more to the point, this imposter deforms reality, while prophetic metaphor "informs" reality. Scripture warns, "Test the spirits." Surrealism insinuates, "Come one and all."

Finally, there is a difference between Western and Eastern transcendence. Eastern mystics and their New Age imitators do deny the self, but even more, they "annihilate"(!) the self—they cease to think, search, feel, or decide. Christian mystics, on the other hand, affirm a "new self" that remains free and aware—not heedless and helpless.

Eastern versions of transcendence seek an imageless and emotionless emptiness, while Western versions embrace both metaphor and emotion. Christianity, for example, "nails to the cross" only those emotions that separate us from God. Our "other" emotions are renewed—not ruined.

As a result, the mystics of Eastern mysticism look at an empty void, while the prophets of *damah* behold a manifest presence. Western art, for example, has long made manifest the otherwise unknown. We find this promise in Plato, Aristotle, Dante, Spenser, Handel, Haydn, Kant, Jaspers, Ricoeur, Whitehead, Dewey, Heidegger, and countless other artists and thinkers.[22]

Finally, Eastern transcendence is totally passive, while Western transcendence is paradoxically active and passive. There is an immense difference, after all, between "floating" mystics and "soaring" prophets.

The list of imitators goes on, but anything other than *damah* gathers fool's gold!

A Holy Holograph

Yet, even *damah* can't put a hammerlock on God's Truth. It reflects, instead, portions of God's Truth. So Paul was right. "We prophecy in part."[23] But with each event of *damah*, additional layers of meanings emerge . . . multiple patterns of significance arise.

There's an old saying, "He who sings prays twice." With endless prophetic metaphor, though, we hear a whole chorus of sacred singers. And God Himself joins this heavenly choir.

These echoing voices prove that worship is not one doctrinal practice, but a polyphonic fugue—multiple melodies weaving soaring similarities. They mean worship is always "happening" . . . never routine or run-of-the-mill. And they imply worship is always reforming . . . not only from what we do, but from what God does.

More important, these voices promise a golden age for the Church in the New Millennium. For the digital medium will allow the greatest kaleidoscope of images and mutations of patterns since the beginning of inspired storytelling.

Yet within this potential, the Church holds an even greater secret over secular society: We are finding that God's Kingdom is a holy holograph. We may prophesy in part, but in His holograph, "the whole is in the part!"

13. MISCARRIED METAPHORS

Still, metaphors do miscarry!

All three dynamics of *damah* must empower worship. Any *damah*—or prophetic metaphor—missing the "known," the "unknown," or the "transcendent," will fail. For prophetic metaphors function under specific spiritual laws. Their rules can be broken. Their language can be misspoken.

And, in our churches, they miscarry more often than not. With painful precision, we now explore the many examples of miscarried metaphors in our worship.

I. The Missing "Known"

Some reformers see tradition as the enemy—the source of all problems. Usually splinter groups, they hold no hope for "worn-out, pointless history." So they consider anything obsolete their big chance. They count any change their big opportunity.

They yearn to break with the past.

Early in this century, the Pentecostalists broke with the past. As cited earlier, they "proclaimed an 'end of history,' a 'new age,' and a 'postmodern era' long before any of these currently fashionable terms were invented."[1] No doubt, they brought a precious move of God to our time. But, then and now, we often miss what the Corinthians missed: We miss our "mind and understanding."[2]

Paul called it "ignorance."[3]

Both fanatic futurists and spirited-filled spiritualists believe being "far-out" is "spiritual."   Often they seek *only* the un-known—the bizarre, the strange, the eccentric, the unearthly. They believe there's method in their madness, but their freedom of "otherness" often becomes the tyranny of "otherness."

And the "known" loses to the "unknown."

But the same miscarried metaphor follows the zealous old as well as the zealous new.   When medieval clergy stubbornly retained the unknown Latin as the official jargon of worship, the Mass turned more and more to mystery . . . the "other" world . . . even superstition.

Archaic and cryptic, religion served up a dark doctrine.

At the same time, the clergy—who staged this mystery—increasingly avoided their followers. They preferred a hierarchy to a body. So they, too, became "dreadful," "sacred," "untouchable." And they "dispensed" salvation.

The "known," as it were, was profaned. And—in many churches—still is.

Without the mediation of the "known"—without a relevance to life—cryptic religions become obscure, silent, empty. . . . And God becomes a Holy Void, a Negative Transcendence, an Absolute Absence, an Infinite Indifference. . . .

Some even say "God is dead."

Chaos, Cacophony, and Vicariism

It would seem only radical reformers and austere liturgists ignore the "known." Not so. Even popular "free" churches refuse it. While an overemphasis on the ascetic leads to "the mystery of the unknown," an overemphasis on freedom leads to "the chaos of the unknown."

"Letting it all hang out."

In the words of Paul, our spirits are no longer in our control.[4] When sublime sense loses touch with common sense, the "unknown" severs from the "known" . . . spontaneity gives way to anarchy . . . and faith cuts loose from its foundation.

There is no frame of reference . . . no way to judge what's going on.

These free flights resemble drug trips. All fire and no effulgence. All vision and no revelation. And their miscarried metaphors point to no reality . . . except, perhaps, Satan himself.

In these churches, the "known" disappears in other ways as well—at times, innocently. In "show-business" services, for example, the full technology of reinforced sound can take natural acoustics already too "alive" and turn them into mind-numbing confusion. Add to this poorly rehearsed and poorly performed music, and we have a cacophony that merely appears to be worship.

It looks and sounds like celebration, but Christ's triumph never arrives!

Finally, if any church were "relevant," it would surely be our market-driven, "seeker sensitive" churches. But the "known" often vanishes here too . . . and no one knows why.

A miscarried metaphor, however, tells us why. The television age has turned everyone into a generation of spectators—the same generation now in church. So during worship, we consign ourselves—like bumps on a log—to watching and listening. The performers up front perform, and worship is rated by how well they do.

Spectator worship, in other words, remains ungrounded in our lives. It may be flashy and immediate on stage, but it remains distant and unknown off stage. Its message is once removed.

It is "vicarious worship."

We must remind ourselves that God is glorified *only* in the Son—in the "Word made flesh." This means the "Word" must also become *our* "flesh." It must become relevant . . . *known*. For only then can God speak to us through prophetic metaphor.

II. The Missing "Unknown"

Though missing the "known" in worship proves tragic, it pales to the missing "unknown." The "unknown" typically disappears when symbols point to themselves . . . when we worship worship . . . when the self-imposed codes of an instilled religious culture become the object of our love.

We worship the medium instead of the message.

At times like these, we find security in the externals of worship . . . the "things" of worship . . . the "traditions" of worship.

They become ends rather than means. Like the worship of beautiful things, their images become "art for the sake of art."

True, all believers rehearse who they are. True, we evaluate, understand, and orient whom we've decided to be. But we step ever so easily over a forbidden line: We magnify our symbols over the power to which they point.

When that happens, worship severs from its Source . . . turns in on itself . . . rules its own small world. And, as a result, mystery reduces to mood. Message forfeits to medium. Dialogue shrinks to monologue. Revelation fades to reveling. And re-creation surrenders to recreation.

These, of course, are idols . . . false fetishes . . . surrogate gods . . . cultic devotions.

Isaiah prophesied the problem: "(They) honor Me with their lips, but remove their hearts and minds far from Me."[5] Jeremiah later explained that trust in outward forms of religion without inward bonds to the Lord is deceptive.[6] And Paul told Timothy these pretenders "hold a form of piety . . . (but) deny and reject and are strangers to the power of it."[7]

We worship the "known" and ignore the "unknown."

The Last Bad Concert

Still, some of us stress "sound traditions" . . . "historical roots" . . . and "ancient practice." We set apart the past as a sacrament itself and ascribe eternal value to its symbols. We pull our ecstasies out of old libraries of sanctity.

. . . as if God would only be happy if we did certain ceremonies in certain ways . . . certain *known* ways.

But historians can't pull spiritual power out of partial metaphors. Raw history and cold theology never have and never will empower worship. In fact—Martin Luther claimed—"The Kingdom of God is not *any* rite."[8]

When we perform only the known past . . . only predictable rites . . . only routine rituals—week after week—tradition turns empty. It follows in the same rut with the ancient Greeks where time becomes a circular treadmill, and nothing new ever gets created.

But adding further insult to injury, the past is not always "good"! After all, human hands have been at work . . . and not always helpfully. That's the reason conductor Toscanini joked, "Tradition is the last bad concert."

More than anything else, Hebrew prophets refused empty formalism. They rejected anything that omitted God. Later, Jesus showed His preference for "a flexible heart" in place of "an inflexible ritual."[9] And when He called us to worship "in spirit and in truth," He excluded "mere external rites."[10]

"Old Manna"

Yet Jesus worshiped in the rites of His day . . . "as was His custom."[11] So what have we missed?

We have missed His distinction between "old manna" and "living bread"[12] . . . between "old metaphor" and "living byword" . . . between powerless symbol and empowered symbol. He knew—and we have forgotten—that metaphors wear out. They lose their power. They turn irrelevant.

In short, they come and go.

Metaphors depend on "newness" for their effect . . . on the "unknown" for their power. What is striking, at first, can lose its surprise later. When history moves beyond old insights . . . when we take outmoded meanings for granted . . . when repeated use wears symbols thin . . . something gets lost.

That something is a figurative language whose figures no longer point to anything transcendent. So, pointless, they turn tired, corny, trite, worn-out. . . .

They become clichés!

But true worship is like a living stream—shifting . . . changing . . . receiving new strength from a thousand tributaries . . . losing old forms in the backwaters of time. Or, true worship is like a great "classic"—enjoyed for a while, then set aside in favor of more prophetic voices.

(Mark Twain jibed, "A classic is something that everybody wants to have read and nobody wants to read.")

Yet, tragically, we believers hold on to our "traditions" long after they have lost their possibility for new life. We retain our religious "things" long after they have become outdated. We find "lasting values" in our routines long past their usefulness.

And when that happens, we lose something far more important than tradition.

Take hymns as example: About three hundred years ago, Isaac Watts reacted to "old and lifeless" psalm singing by giving birth to today's hymn singing. But Watts' idea stirred great conflict among mainline Protestants, for this "new" music was not part of the church's past.

After awhile, of course, the tables turned. Today, hymn tunes, cast in the semi-morbid harmonies of the nineteenth-century, sound inane to ears toughened on twentieth century tonalities. And texts like "Bring forth the royal diadem" strike listeners under fifty as "gobbledygook."

Still, in the fight between traditional hymns and popular choruses, both sides are losing. The correct controversy is not between traditional and popular tastes. It is between living and dead metaphors—old or new!

The Newest "Known"

For routine rituals and common clichés are not limited to the past. We also know the shallow known—and suffer the missing "unknown"—in the newest consumer-driven churches. We trace this shallowness, in fact, to the latest entertainment-driven society.

This century shifted toward "mass culture" as entertainment giants became the primary providers of information. And mass entertainment profits—more than anything else—drive the world today. Everyone is into the "latest and greatest." Everyone is into "style and stuff." And everyone loves a "good show."

Church leaders see this, of course; and the smart ones look for things that "work." So they copy the latest fads—whatever meets popular opinion . . . whatever finds favor . . . whatever the market requires to attract and hold their potential flock.

And congregations respond alike. The "new and improved" drives our addiction. The latest craze creates our hunger. The "next," the "newest," the "now" runs our hidden tyranny.

The fire of fads has replaced the fire of faith.

And the results?   Services have become entertainment events . . . Christian variety shows . . . sixty-minute "infomercials." The better the "performers," the greater the "anointing." Of course, there is nothing wrong with this if all the gimmicks and glitter support a prophetic metaphor.

Usually, they don't!

Then, the entertainment world also requires its stars . . . its personalities . . . its pumped-up leaders. The church, after all, must do the same! So our clerical stars learn to "turn on" their "glory groupies." They learn to rig their worship. They learn to elicit their show-business goals. And, perhaps, there is nothing wrong with this if their egos bow to a prophetic metaphor.

Often, they don't!

Finally, entertainment moves our emotions . . . pushes our buttons . . . rings our bells. But this comes as no surprise to a "celebration" church where theology centers on emotion in the first place. These believers easily seek emotions. They naturally flow with passions. They effortlessly exalt excitement. And, of course, there is nothing wrong with this if they know the difference between spiritual and natural emotions.

Frequently, they don't.

In the absence of the "unknown," all this veneer means showing up not only "in the world" but "of the world" . . . disguising secular styles with sacred apparel . . . exalting dazzling symbols above deeper signs.

Too often, the church embraces the "known" while refusing the "unknown."

Overnight Clichés

The "new," after all, is not always new. Celebration-style churches can slip into empty ritual just as easily with praise choruses as with older hymns. The latest fads can become overnight clichés.

That's the reason Martin Luther feared "fickly" spirits "who delight only in novelty and tire of it as quickly when it has worn off."

In the first place, pop art—of necessity—must come with simple and easy pleasure. This trait does not prevent profundity, but it usually manifests a cosmetic, neutered, Muzak version of the real thing. It usually means no one is challenged and no one is changed.

And—agreed—no harm done. But, when leaders bring this known simplicity into the church without the prophetic gift of the "unknown," God's message becomes trivial. It becomes impotent . . . much the way the commercial "swing" of white musicians in the thirties cheapened the spiritual profundity of black jazz from the twenties.

The "known"—by itself—is a human idea. It is not prophetic at all. When great paradigms appear, mere appearances disappear. There's a difference, after all, between secular "trends" and sacred "transformations."

For finally, prophetic metaphors are *for* us. They are not *of* us, or *by* us.

> "We stand in Christ's presence when we speak; God looks us in the face. We get what we say straight from God and say it as honestly as we can."[13]

"Merging, Blending, Synthesizing, and Converging"

One renewal movement tries to avoid this tyranny of the new . . . this triteness of the novel. It seeks to resolve the issue by combining the old with the new. It enhances its vision by blending one style with another.

It's called "convergence" worship.

Openly recognized about 1985, mainstream churches now bring together two streams of worship: liturgical and charismatic. The movement could claim to be ecumenical except few evangelical, fundamental, or charismatic churches participate.

Convergence worship seeks to combine freedom with form . . . to merge power with pattern . . . to balance trends with tradition. And Scripture supports these desires:

> Every teacher and interpreter of the Sacred Writings . . . is like a householder who brings forth out of his storehouse treasure that is new and [treasure that is] old [the fresh as well as the familiar].[14]

Yet worthy goals can miss the mark. A simple synthesis of old and new fails to preserve their vital difference. A bland blending of diverse styles fails to protect their rare diversity. And the mere merging of conflicting traditions fails to conserve their original powers.

Boiling down this broth loses the meat of each form. Lowering differences to the lowest denominators hides the paradox in each pattern. Knocking the rough edges off knocks the raw enigma off each tradition.

These neutered visions are like television which seldom embodies truth because it is a mere consensus of truth. Our consensus, after all, leaves old errors in place and ignores the move of God in our time. And our hoped-for power of a Pentecost simply melts into one more formal liturgy.

After all, a prophetic metaphor does not "merge," "blend," "synthesize" or "converge." Instead, it "compares" . . . "juxtaposes" . . . "contrasts" . . . "holds things in tension." Revelation, in other words, comes only when diverse worship traditions retain their pristine, untranslated, unreduced forms. We may place them side-by-side in their full integrity and raw conflict, but we never "converge" them.

"Convergence" may be the wrong banner for this worthy movement.

III. The Missing "Transcendence"

A transcendent message provides the final proof of a prophetic metaphor. Yet, how frequently we prevent it. Typically, we turn ongoing revelation into static dogma. We force intuitive feelings into legal reasonings. We push embryonic images into codified canons.

We "shoot" this fluttering creature in flight with the quick triggers of analysis, judgment, and extracted answers.

Prophetic metaphors require a gestation period . . . a time of meditative reflection . . . a quiet movement from hidden spirit to conscious mind. In the words of Blaise Pascal, these are "reasons of the heart, for which reason knows nothing." If we move too quickly to evaluate these visions, we analyze only half-discovered truths.

This is the source of the error: The Reformation reacted to medieval mystery by exalting the role of the intellect. Then the Enlightenment (1700-1950) viciously stripped away any remaining mystery. So, today, culture demands quickly converting the tension between the "known" and the "unknown" into an acceptable theology.

For reason must remain supreme.

But this only calls forth our known world . . . our biased blindness . . . our particular prejudice . . . "the word of [mere] men."[15] Or, in the words of Voltaire, "the lie commonly agreed upon."

Typically, churches ignore transcendence when form refuses freedom . . . when heavy-handed authority determines truth . . . when the sermon serves the main focus of worship . . . and when silence becomes an enemy.

As a result, worship becomes a precisely defined liturgy . . . the propaganda of aspiring priests in a worldly theocracy . . . an intellectual assent to refined rhetoric . . . and a wall-to-wall busyness of sights and sounds.

It might easily be called "ordained spiritual amnesia."

And it happens everywhere. Both liberals and fundamentalists mirror the same rationalist system that reduces God to practical
proportions. Both groups deny the mystery. Both groups deny the
"transcendent."

Finally, each denomination becomes its own little world . .
. its own small ghetto. Then, century upon century, layer upon
layer, accretions are added. Worship becomes a fossil hidden
beneath endless strata of hardened dogma.

In the end, refusing transcendence is an act of pride. But
Saint Paul cried the more critical alarm: "Reason without the Holy
Spirit . . . is death."[16]

Visible Sails and Invisible Wind

In summary, let us affirm once more the "known," the
"unknown," and the "transcendent" in worship.

The "known," after all, is us! But when we dress in
religious "clothes" and give ourselves the starring role in our
religious drama, we resemble mere actors practicing in front of a
mirror.

So we also require the "unknown," the "not-us." More to
the point, we require the tension between the "known" and the "not-
us." This tension is like the shoreline between an island and the
endless sea. Or, it is like a visible sailboat pulled by an invisible
wind.

We must resist limiting our soul to one or the other.

The issue of worship, for example, is not a matter of style
or liturgy. Or, as the Quakers put it, "(Worship) stands neither in

forms nor in the formal disuse of forms." In short, the eternal in our work doesn't make the work itself eternal.

Styles come and go. Metaphors appear and disappear.

Nor is "renewed" worship a mere matter of doing something different . . . repackaging the old . . . making the old "new." For the "different" does not always contradict the "known." The "repackaged" does not always inspire paradox.

A broken metaphor is a broken metaphor regardless of how "trendy."

The issue is a "live" metaphor—both human and divine . . . visible and invisible . . . active and contemplative . . . ancient and new . . . science and art. Yes, art! Hebrew *damah*—our prophetic metaphor—was a holy art. And today's worship requires the same artistic skills.

"A Holy Art"

But there is no art—no worship—without risk . . . without sacrifice. We must risk transcending the environment we're in . . . turning our backs on the pious paraphrases of the past . . . separating the mutable from the immutable.

Then, we must risk the "unknown" with the "known" . . . the awe with the ordinary . . . the mystery with the mundane . . . the intuitive with the intellect. For everything that glides across God's face must take on the qualities of the "unknowable."

This means bold responses to divine inspiration. For too long, great worship meant following the right rules. But great worship differs in no way from great art where breakthroughs come from knowing where to break rules.

Then, imagination gives form to inspiration. Or, in the words of Shakespeare, "Imagination bodies forth the forms of things unknown." And, like faith, it gives "substance," "evidence," and "proof" to them.[17]

Again, it's the "Word made flesh."

Sometimes prophetic leaders create new metaphors, and sometimes they reawaken old ones. Rare is the metaphor so powerful that it needs no awakening. Rare is the metaphor that remains an eternal, living instrument. And rare is the metaphor that deepens with repetition.

So most metaphors—not created anew—live in a realm of suspended animation and must be reawakened. Worship leaders, then, must resemble musicians who avoid playing the same music in the same wearisome way.

Our God is the Great Creator—not the "Great Imitator." And He created us in His image. So we were created to create and, then, re-created to re-create. New creatures, in other words, always create new things.[18]   God refuses our desire for yesterday's "manna."[19]

Endlessly He commands, "Behold, I am doing a new thing! Now it springs forth; do you not perceive and know it and will you not give heed to it?"[20]

And Paul echoes, "Don't become so well-adjusted to your culture that you fit into it without even thinking."[21] And "Don't think that you can be wise merely by being up-to-date with the times."[22]

So all wisdom—old and new—is saying the same thing. Shouldn't our hope for the New Millennium Church seem obvious? Shouldn't our desire for *damah* seem essential?

V. THE PERIL

14. FEELING OUR WAY

All the metaphors are propelling the same motive. All the trends are projecting the same intent. All the streams are plunging into the same river.

This motive . . . this intent . . . this river . . . is "emotion."

Indeed, "emotion"—or "feelings"—will decide future reality and totally reshape religion in the twenty-first century.

The Death of Disembodied Minds

Predictions like these are absurd, of course . . . at least for "civilized" minds (like ours!). Because Descartes—the father of modern minds—taught: "true knowledge comes only from reason . . . don't trust your senses . . . feelings are mere base impulses."

And, taking this logic further, modern scientists conclude, "If emotion is not a 'thing,' it is in effect nothing!"

So the "educated" have learned to master their emotions . . . to divorce fact from fervor . . . to seek an "intellectual" ecstasy (if that's possible). And even reformed church leaders urge their flock to keep sacred senses to a "safe level" . . . to prefer a "pure" faith . . . to keep the mind "undefiled" by feelings.

Typical is Kierkegaard's comment:

A beautiful feeling should be "fully affirmed and enjoyed," but we must keep it "in its proper place." So under such restraints, dying denominational churches reduce passions to "reports of passions."

They read spiritual cookbooks to a starving public.

But these "modern"ideas are gone. The cold logic of the print tradition . . . the sterile faith of cerebral churches . . . and the smug apathy of schooled scholars are now past history.

They are "*post*modern." Now, we realize the "death of God" notion was actually "the death of disembodied minds"—minds separated from intuitive and emotional wisdom.

So today, visionary scholars dare to say, "Emotion lies at the very root of civilization" and remains "central to the issues of modern times"[1] . . . that "Emotions, not IQ, may be the true measure of human intelligence"[2] . . . and that "Emotion is central to the process of rational thought."[3]

Our senses, after all, are not "nonsense."

Life is bigger than logic. Without feeling, nothing matters. For reality is personal . . . it is *felt*. And the relevance of reality is even more personal . . . it is even *more* felt.

> Most agree that we are entering a period in which we will see the world and ourselves less cerebrally and more intuitively, less analytically and more immediately, less literally and more analogically.[4]

A New Paradigm

Television hurried the demise of cold logic. We not only "see" the image on the screen, we also "feel" we are seeing it. Our lives are shaped by these hidden senses. Indeed, early TV mixed these feelings with the sentiments of feel-good, sixties hippies and the emotions of pentecostalism to birth an entirely new church.

It was a potent recipe!

Early on, we found the "content" of television through our experience and its "meaning" through our response. Then, into this pot, history stirred the life style of the early boomers. Their free-love, spontaneity, narcissism, and do-your-own-thing mysticism, blended perfectly with the new medium.

And, ready in the wings, stood the—until now—alien theology of Holy Spirit revivals. This ancient—yet new—idea insists that God is *not* an idea. Instead, the centerpiece of this theology is *emotion.* Its believers knew that New Testament worship was not possible without the Holy Spirit. More important, this "manifest" presence still touches our deepest emotions.

Of course, these conspiring trends—television, the '60's youth, and Holy Spirit revivals—created a new church . . . a new paradigm church that has touched every believer on every continent and continues to outpace every other tradition.

Its worship moves with emotion.

Virtual Passions

But the story is not over. Today, the '90's youth and the digital age are both moving toward an emotional reality unknown even today. The young already know visceral images in their movies, videos, and CD's that have forever closed the gap between spirit and body . . . mind and emotion.

These forever changed kids have already replaced objective facts with raw experience . . . ordained doctrines with altered states . . . literal statements with sensory intuition . . . logical sequence with multimedia metaphors. And their turned-on world moves so mightily, they even require time-outs to "chill-out."

In short, they anticipate the digital age:

"Personal computers" will become more "personal" than ever imagined. The digital age will become more sensory than ever believed. In short, it will prove a supremely sensual, multisensory, virtual-realty, multimedia world.

This new multimedia, for example, will prove no ordinary multimedia. Instead, it will be a virtual hall of emotional mirrors . . . a kaleidoscope of sensory images . . . a meditation of multiple metaphors. Indeed, we will look back on today's movies the way we now look back on yesterday's silent movies.

Already, digital innovation—not possible without emotion—drives the world economy. After all, intuitive visions and inspired feelings deeply require each other, and the profit motive only deepens that bond. Amy Lowell wrote, for example, "Whatever (creativity) is, emotion, apprehended or hidden, is a part of it." For "Only emotion can rouse the subconscious into action."

So the creative future and our prophetic passions will doubtless walk hand in hand.

Yet many disagree! They complain that digital sensory experience is only *virtual* reality—not really real! But what's new about that? Every art form . . . ritual . . . symbol . . . or metaphor is "virtual." Their hidden feelings all represent something "not there"—something beyond themselves. And, no doubt, computers will continue crunching numbers, but these numbers will increasingly become the viscera of our passions—in the same way that film science now moves the moods in our movies.

We've got to get beyond this silliness. The very future of the Church depends on our ability to proclaim passionate metaphors—or vital "virtual realities"—in the coming age.

"Clouds Without Water"

So emotion—for better or worse—becomes the underlying theme of the twenty-first century. Though the mind and will always play integral parts, all the trends—postmodernism, the new paradigm church, the New Millennium youth, and the new multisensory, virtual reality future—point to a new role for emotion.

But it's an emotion without definition . . . without guidelines . . . without caution. When this happens, cutting edge congregations can claim anything in the name of their feelings.

Such liberty waves an alarming flag, and so far, everyone has missed it! All of our moods—love, joy, pride, anger, fear, jealousy, sorrow, or solitude—arise from either natural, spiritual, or demonic sources.[5] To confuse them is to court disaster.

Scripture is clear.

With lucid caution, Jesus commands Peter to recognize the difference between natural and spiritual love.[6] And, writing to Christians, Paul purposely points to a "zeal and enthusiasm for God" that's *wrong*![7] Further, he rebukes "desires that spring from delusion,"[8] and asks, "Why does your heart carry you away?"[9]

Here is a modern example of being "carried away":

Pride proves a typical culprit among the "pillars of the church." Granted, there is a "spiritual" pride,[10] but natural pride always calls the things of God its own. My doctrine! My church! My pew! It's even proud of its own humility. And, "wise in its own eyes," it quickly sees faults in others.[11]

Further, this natural self-esteem often effects a show. It courts attention. Jesus said, "Take care not to do your good deeds . . . in order to be seen."[12] But vanity only "takes care" of itself. It shows a form of godliness—Paul said—but without power.[13]

So it creates its own power. It talks big. Its religious rhetoric flows fluent, fervent, and fulsome. Jonathan Edwards called it "ostentatious hypocrisy," and Scripture likened such self-righteous blowhards to "clouds without water, swept along by the winds."[14]

Yet, this mood is no anomaly from the norm. Pompous opinions are always within us and around us. We are often "vainly puffed up by (our) sensuous notions and inflated by (our) unspiritual thoughts and fleshly conceit."[15]

We often fall victim to "religious" emotions.

A Shooting Gallery

From the start, the church battled this three-headed monster. For emotion—like imagination—sins as much as it saves . . . it distorts as much as it discloses . . . and it lies as much as it verifies. It's no surprise, then, we've inherited a love/hate story toward our feelings. The same preachers on the same day will say, "I can just *feel* the presence of God," then later warn, "Don't give in to your emotions—you can't trust them."

(Perhaps we shouldn't blame these preachers. The raging underground seas of raw religious feelings have terrified them, and the fickle passions of their followers have burned scars into their clerical skins.)

Often our confused emotions trace to the word "soul":

The "soul"—in English—was never the Judeo-Christian "soul." It is a Greek soul! But the Greek idea of soul is "just what *The New Testament* does not teach."[16] And it is "equally misleading" in the *Old Testament*.[17] So we remain confused about our most critical concern—our real self.

Even in church!

We confuse soul with spirit because they are both immaterial. They both contrast a material body. So we modern Greeks mistakenly call our soul "the real self—the everlasting self." But the Hebrew "soul"—on its own—is just the opposite! It is only natural. It is godless human nature.[18] It has no hope for heaven without clinging to a renewed spirit. In fact, Jesus said the only way we can "save our soul" is to "lose it"![19]

Between our soul and spirit, then, we partly seek evil and partly seek good. Part of us loves sin, and part of us hates it. So in a sense, we have a split personality. Two persons live in us, and both are trying to kill each other!—one for the wrong reason, the other for the right reason.

Indeed, our inner ecstasy is a shooting gallery!

Spiritual Fornication

But it doesn't have to be this way. We simply can't see our emotional source. As a result, we don't know if it is God's power or our power . . . Spirit led or lying manipulation . . . unselfish or selfish . . . faith or flesh . . . eternal or temporal.

We can't tell, for example, a commanding coercion from an inspired call, or a desperate craving from a tender yearning. We can't distinguish passion from compassion, luring from longing, or an impetuous demand from a compelling desire.

We can't separate a master-craftsman from an anointed artist, or dazzling skill from a moment of true power. We can't discern a show business shyster from a legitimate leader, or an enormous ego from an eternal vision.

So hot on the heels of false emotion comes false fact. We pass off phony feelings for pure passions. We counterfeit "religious" affections for spiritual ecstasy. We burn cheap, natural "fuels" in our "spirit-led" hearts.

Hebrew writers called it "spiritual fornication," for our mistaken love catches only a glimpse of true love.[20]

Then, finally, deeper calamities hide in ambush. Spiritual leaders with inflated natural emotions—or even demonic emotions!—easily imagine make-believe "visions" from God. And, without accountability, their delusions create tragedies.

"Self-Made Fires"

Whether "religious" or not, the natural soul is driven by human nature alone . . . just as it is . . . untouched by anything spiritual or supernatural.[21]   In fact, natural emotions are "nonspiritual." Though suave and stylish among the elegant elite, these innate instincts remain flesh and blood urges . . . garden variety motives . . . knee-jerk desires.

They are only mirrored images of us . . . "self-made fires" . . . monologues of human desires.[22] Jesus came to the point: "Flesh gives birth to flesh."[23]

We might patiently accept these traits . . . but for one problem: Natural emotions can't reach God. They are "incapable of knowing (God)"![24] Worse still, they are "opposed" to God; and God is "opposed" to them![25]

What are these commonly shared sentiments? And how do we recognize them?

Narcotic Deceptions

First, we recognize natural emotions because they're selfish. They begin and end with self-interest. Self-seeking lives inbreed self-centeredness, self-preservation, and self-pleasure. They may "look good"—even altruistic!—and they may feel snug and secure in the warm embrace of religion. But the needs of the self remain the primary purpose.

Next, natural emotions nail us to the environment. Random incidents demand our response. Daily events oversee our obsessions. For by definition, these flesh and blood feelings respond "to factors outside the individual—circumstances in his environment."[26]

That's the reason these instincts always manifest tunnel vision. They always operate within narrow contexts. They always pursue small things with impatience while ignoring large things with indifference.

They "paint small pictures."

In the same way, they are short-lived—on, then off . . . hot, then cold . . . "yes," then "no." In other words, they are fleeting, fickle, and, finally, futile! In fact, the very meaning of natural emotion implies a "short-lived reaction"[27] or "the temporary element in human nature."[28]

In worship, this emotion compares to the affect of alcohol on the body: "Tipsy" sentimentalists are "spiritual" while the warm fire of emotion burns. But when the "alcohol" of their affections wears off, their feelings turn icy cold, and they fall quickly into unbelief.

So it's evident that natural emotions have an "unreality" about them. Their narcotic deceits pretend something they are not. They assume postures without import.[29] Or, Scripture calls them only "outward and seeming."[30] For, again, the meaning of natural emotion includes "that which is merely external or only apparent, in opposition to what is spiritual and real."[31]

Plastic and Cosmetic

Perhaps the greatest historical tragedies occur, though, when clever leaders manipulate our natural emotions. For we blithely submit to any and everything. We accept as fact all suggestions. We easily become enthralled . . . spellbound . . . consumed . . . even enslaved.

We are, after all, "plastic."

All leaders—secular and sacred—must "move" their followers, and swaying them often means exploiting their emotions. So these leaders have one rule: "If it works, do it!" But exploiting other's feelings—even for "good ends"—is a mistake. If we maneuver them toward worthy goals, it is just as likely someone else will move them toward unworthy goals.

By example, the very word "sentimentality" means "forced feeling." It is a pumped up, theatrical hype. It spreads by overt overstatement, compelling contagion, and cagey counterfeit. These skills conceal cunning . . . but, in the worldly realm, they always work. We resemble Pavlov's dogs—drooling at the ring of a bell.

We drivel emotions we don't even have!

Finally, however, the greatest spiritual tragedies result from an even viler negative: We never change. No effort of natural emotion can redeem the darkened human soul. Even under the guise of religion, these instincts achieve zero spiritual growth.

In fact, they resist change.

We may "improve" ourselves with the human tools of a natural world. We may alter or control our natural passions. We may even wax evermore refined. But our heroic "newness" never penetrates beyond the natural soul.

It is a cosmetic change.

The Enemy of Worship

So natural emotion is the enemy of worship . . . a deceptive trap . . . a dangerous ecstasy. It's like a drugged society seeking "God-in-a-Pill." Even noble goals . . . romantic ideas . . . poetic visions . . . or burning passions remain natural if their source is natural.

Jonathan Edwards called these instincts "exceedingly different and immensely inferior" to spiritual emotions.

And no one escapes. Everyone possesses—and is possessed by—natural emotions. There is a purpose in this reality after all. Fear avoids the threats to our lives, and sex claims a future for our genes.

We survive!

But survival is not enough. Paul warned his converts, "Are you not unspiritual and of the flesh, behaving yourselves after a human standard and like mere (unchanged men)?"[32] So he said we must "*habitually* put to death" our old ways and be "*constantly* renewed."[33] Then God's "tender compassions" can be "new *every* morning."[34]

In short, our natural soul must die daily. We must live endless lives of benevolent deaths.

Testing the Spirits

By now, we know not all emotion is natural. But not all "spirit-inspired" emotion is godly, either. Some of it is demonic! Since seraph and snake abide side by side in the realm of spirit, a "move of the spirit" may not be a good thing. Some moods are maladies. Some passions are polluted. Some sentiments are sinister.

That's the reason we must "be vigilant and cautious at all times."[35] We must test the spirits "to discover whether they proceed from God."[36] Then, we must "hold fast . . . (to) what is good."[37]

Yet, few do this.

Whatever we call it—evil, Satan, the demonic—the signs remain the same. This sadistic shadow always conspires to destroy us . . . usually with deception. We step into this deceit—like quicksand—unintended and unsuspected.

We find natural thrills, for example, entirely normal. But too often, these thrills come from "thrillers"—books about murder . . . films about violence. Then, we fall ever easily for darker "kicks." Or, we often mistake our natural anger for righteous anger, then—without our knowing—it twists into demonic hate. History abounds, for example, with heresy hunters who become the very devils they hate.

None are immune! Just think how many reputations are murdered over teacups. And our courteous swords never feel the wounds.

Yes, even in church! Under a "religious" facade, evil can imitate truth . . . it can mimic virtue . . . it can twist spirituality.

William James, for example, described a "diabolical mysticism"—a religious mysticism turned upside down. This deceit didn't surprise Paul: "Satan himself masquerades as an angel of light." So "It is not surprising if (Satan's) servants also masquerade as ministers of righteousness."[38]

Today, we think how ridiculous it was for Satan to quote Scripture to Jesus. But it wasn't ridiculous then! Or, consider Jesus' own disciples when the crowds refused their master, "Lord, do You wish us to command fire to come down from heaven and consume them?" But Jesus revealed the evil spirit in their "fire": "You do not know of what sort of spirit you are, for the Son of man did not come to destroy men's lives."[39]

Are we more sophisticated? Have we risen above this ancient past? Then recall that our own church supported slavery in the South.

Ignoring demonic emotions is like trying to erase our shadow. But if we recognize and resist these moods, James said, They will "flee from you."[40]

Neglected Truth

If we only renew our understanding of emotion, we will not be "destroyed for a lack of knowledge."[41] For, unlike natural or demonic moods, spiritual emotions carry no inherent errors or forewarned limits.

For "Spirit gives birth to spirit."[42] In other words, spiritual emotions respond only to Spirit. They are shared sentiments . . . vicarious feelings . . . "not-me" emotions. They rejoice solely in what His Spirit likes and scorn only what His Spirit rejects.

"Faith and its consequent joy," for example "do not come from ourselves." "This joy has its source beyond mere earthly, human joy . . . it is thus a spiritual gift."[43] In the same way, "Love . . . (springs) from God." Our "earnest zeal and care" are "planted" by God. All these feelings, and many more, result from "the work which His presence within accomplishes."[44]

Spiritual emotion, then, means more as a messenger . . . a medium . . . a mediator between the life of the senses and the life of the spirit. By analogy, only muscles move us when we exercise the natural body, but hidden powers propel the ecstatic dancer.

These emotions are easy to recognize. They are self-less—meek, mild, modest, and merciful. Yet, they rise above the moment . . . they remain free of circumstance . . . they move beyond the chances and changes of small lives. Tillich described them as both "infinite passion and passion for the infinite."

More important, Spiritual emotion is a "knowing" emotion . . . a felt meaning . . . a wisdom of the heart. It yields light with its heat . . . revelation with its warmth . . . insight with its inspiration. Even in moments of enigma or paradox, these feelings perceive the truth: Spiritual joy always recalls a taste of bitter in its sweet-ness—it triumphs only in relation to what was overcome. And "Godly grief . . . never brings regret"—it always contains a seed of hope.[45]

That's the reason Paul could wildly assert, "Let us rejoice in our sufferings."[46]

Faith, after all, requires spiritual emotion. Hope means "the joyful anticipation of our desire." And faith is "activated . . . energized . . . (and) expressed . . . through love."[47] The very meaning of faith confirms it: "Faith is the assurance (that is, the heartfelt encouragement) . . . of things [we] hope for." Further, it is "the conviction (that is, the fervent belief) of their reality."[48]

This is not new truth, but neglected truth.

———— •••◉••• ————

A new language is emerging out of the ashes of modernism. It is decidedly the language of metaphor. It will decidedly ride a wave of emotion.

No longer must spiritual emotion be kept in its "proper place"—its place will be pervasive. No longer must sanctified mood be confined to its limited role—its role will be inclusive. And no longer can we dismiss pure intuition as "just feeling"—its feeling will speak the language of prophetic metaphor.

So let's reclaim the power of our passion . . . before it's too late!

"I am He Who searches . . . feelings . . . and the [inmost] hearts, and I will give to each of you [the reward for what you have done] as your work deserves."[49]

15. DIGITAL DEMONS

Hidden in the Hypertext

This is a book of faith. Faith in the future of a digital world. These pages see a Creator-God moving in a new and loving way. These words see a New Millennium Church enjoying the best of its day.

Yet, with the unaware, the facts also foretell a more ominous future.

For the digital age predicts both triumph and tragedy . . . promise and peril . . . victories and victims. The end of modernity may free us from worn-out versions of history and outdated renderings of reality, but it also exposes us to frightening risks of fatality.[1]

Already, the Internet—a model of the future—evolves with nobody in charge. Its inventors admit that it is out of control . . . that its offspring are totally untamed. And hidden in the hypertext, endless deceits and destructions await the digital church.

In truth, demonic forces seem already to hold the higher ground.

A Digital Deity

All darkness begins as light. Let's face it, modern science has solved many problems, and the belief that it will solve even more problems is entirely reasonable. Even irresistible. Maybe "the answer to everything!" Certainly, we can understand why we look to technology even for deliverance.

It's our story! We have reduced spirit to mind, mind to brain, brain to computer, and computer to machine. And now, machines—potentially "perfect vessels"—must come to the aid of our imperfect vessels . . . especially if we are to reap the fruit of our dreams:

> We can control the destiny of the world. We can extend our will—all-knowing and ever-present —across the vast reaches of our race. And we can do it through the limitless freedom of pure digital intelligence.

But there's a flip side. The machine can take over! Marshall McLuhan wrote, "We shape our tools, and thereafter our tools shape us." And Jacques Ellul echoed, "Technology, as a tool, transforms itself into technology as master."

The famous computer, "Deep Blue," for example, finally beat the world's top chess player, Gary Kasparov. And this triumph will happen in every aspect of life . . . including religion. Computers, however, "are not moral; they cannot resolve complex issues like the rights to life and to death."[2] Yet, we will more and more rely on computers for value judgments, the way we now rely on calculators for our forgotten math skills.

We'll simply cling to larger crutches.

As this reliance finally turns, though, to submission, we serve the tool instead of the tool serving us. And, as we confuse judgments of probability with judgements of value, "We mix good and evil, right and wrong, and make space for the absolute triumph of absolute Evil in the world."[3]

In the words of Lochhead, we turn "our attempts at self-salvation into instruments of alienation and oppression . . . (and this) imagined means of deliverance results only in our greater bondage."[4]

Clearly, a digital deity looms on the horizon.

Technology and Magic

And it's not easy to discern this deity from a demon. Computers can fool us.

In the first place, they are attractive . . . seductive . . . addictive. And their beguiling pleasures easily manipulate the mind and spirit. Let's admit it, computer software often seems "magical." Indeed, its proclaimed "power" actually blurs the boundary between technology and magic.[5]

Moreover, it poses as anything or anyone it wants to be. It's possible, for example, to totally mask your identity on a computer, and the person at the other end would never know. Such anonymity plants wild deceit.

Or, in the words of Scripture, the "tares" never get separated from the "wheat."

In this "virtual reality," we must learn the difference, then, between illusions and metaphors. Illusions deceive; metaphors disclose. Illusions listen to the powers of darkness. Prophetic metaphors hear the voice of God.

The Wild Web

So discernment is critical. On the Internet, freedom reigns
. . . anything goes . . . nothing is forbidden. In fact, the computer
culture has "a nearly mystical faith in the benign force of uninhib-
ited information."[6]

Grateful Dead lyricist and Internet enthusiast John Perry
Barlow put it this way:

> Cyberspace, in its present condition, has a lot in
> common with the 19th century West. It is vast,
> unmapped, culturally and legally ambiguous . . .
> hard to get around in, and up for grabs. Large
> institutions already claim to own the place, but most
> of the actual natives are solitary and independent,
> sometimes to the point of sociopathy. It is, of
> course, a perfect breeding ground for both outlaws
> and new ideas about liberty.[7]

This new "wild west" on the World Wide Web means
problems for the church. Slowly but surely, a do-it-yourself, pick-
and-choose spirituality is tearing down the ideological walls and
spiritual gates of the traditional church. "Off-line" as well as "on-
line," we are seeing the "complete deconstruction of the whole
value system."[8] And it's occurring at "warp velocity."[9]

Already, "Christianity is anathema to postmodernists."[10]
And the Internet is openly called a "clearinghouse of contemporary
heresy."[11] In fact, the reigning beliefs of cyber-culture are plainly
post-Christian.[12]

The values of church, family, and state no longer provide
the window on the world . . . no longer restrain behavior . . . no

longer supply moral authority. In truth, opinions are shaped more by the entertainment industry than by the traditional institutions of society.

And—contrary to Washington's "spin doctors"—the values we're now deciding have little to do with democracy. Democracy is rule by the people. Here, there are no rules.

It's called anarchy.

Everyone's an Editor

Even before the digital age, we were suffering from the "relativity" of truth. Secular scientists assumed that the theory of relativity and quantum mechanics applied to all things—including society. Since scientific reality changes according to how we look at it, they took for granted that values change too.

As a result, today's truth is relative. Our opinions come first, then the justification for them. To be more honest, we base faith and facts on what's-in-it-for-us.

We create them. And they, in turn, create us.

This fickle falsehood is bad enough, but now, the digital age will "reinvent" truth on a scale never seen before. For digital reality is amazingly plastic. It can alter text at a whim . . . it can reinvent reality in a second . . . it can redefine "truth" with caprice.

Indeed, we are our own editors.

No longer will the great "classics" of art and literature, for example, stand on their own. Supposedly complete and unalterable

art will be edited by each observer for a more personally appealing
finish.[13] [14]

Nothing is safe. Nothing is sacred.

A Collective Fantasy

And, though each will edit reality, we will still end up with
a "collective" truth. Though each will refer to local standards, we
will still end up with "global" standards. For the Internet is a
paradoxical warp that creates conformists out of a mass of separat-
ists. In other words, our values will rise from a "collage" of beliefs
. . . a "consensus" of concerns . . . an "assimilation" of information.

A collective consciousness.

It will give the look of unity, but—like Babel—it will prove
disunity. We will seek an accord, but—like baloney—we will bite
into the cheapest, anything-goes meat: A ground-down, one-world
spirituality . . . no religion more credible than another . . . no
"spirit" more believable than another.

The final orthodoxy . . . and the final heresy.

For better or worse, this collective fantasy will force the
church to change. It will also weaken the nation-state, for it will
create unavoidable conflicts with traditional power structures.
Indeed, violence may prove intrinsic to this transition.

Tapscott calls it "The New World (Dis)Order."

An Unimproved End

Computers may evolve the power to rule, but we are the ones who feed the monster. So without redeemed souls, the digital future will rise to no greater level than us! When we empower ourselves to "edit the world," we also empower ourselves to destroy the world.

After all, computers are simply possibility machines. They model the future and bring it to pass. They amplify our will and create global results. They exaggerate human nature and imprint it on everybody.

At a staggering rate!

But the computer cannot compensate for fallen human nature—"imperfect man, who is never free of pride, self-interest, envy, vanity, and dozens of other defects."[15] For years, we celebrated the idea that we were infallible . . . that we were naturally good and open to endless progress . . . that we would forever transform and transcend ourselves.

But history made this myth mad. The facts bear witness to our infinite capacity to turn everything we touch into tools of death. "Our inventions," Thoreau wrote, "are but improved means to an unimproved end."

So computers only magnify the errors in the errant human will. They only empower the fallen in a fallen world.

"Be not deceived, God is not mocked; for whatsoever a man soweth, that shall he also reap."[16]

Garbage at the Speed of Light

Quests for godlike powers among unredeemed minds will lead us to the dark side of cyberspace. Computer-nerds, cyber-punks, and misfit technocrats will be tempted to control those less informed. In their hands, the computer will become a tool of privilege to manipulate those less privileged.

Our dream of equal access to the digital future could easily prove wrong. In its place, we would see a sinister new Darwin-ism—a satanic survival of the fittest. We would see a bipolar world of "haves" and "have-nots" . . . a two-tiered separation of "knowers" and "know-nots."

Information apartheid.

Such tyrannies would probably spawn electronic mobs . . . gangs of geeks . . . digital insurgents. Then, in response, watchdog governments would willingly attack those threats. Computer-savvy civil servants would gladly enter forbidden places. And cold technocrats would love turning us into numbers.

Real-time surveillance would be real. The invasion of personal privacy would be irrevocable. The computer, after all, has a chilling potential to know everything about us.

In fact, It already does. The future is here!

Already, we see the dangers and depravities on the Internet—obscene sex, hate literature, on-line crime . . . indeed, "toxic levels of information-sewage."[17] Already the social decay of this nation speeds uninvited down the information highway into the still remaining, wholesome homes of other cultures.

It's garbage at the speed of light.

An Instrument of the Spirit

So we're the problem, not the computer. In trying to conquer the threats of the computer, we're really trying to conquer ourselves.

The creative visions of computer technology began in the Spirit, but Paul saw our wrong response centuries ago: "Are you so foolish? After beginning in the Spirit, are you now trying to attain your goal by human effort?"[18]

So—on behalf of the world—the Church should claim this new gift as a blessing of the Spirit, not a tool of soulish pride. The Church should insist on equal access to this empowered future, not a separation of the "haves" and "have-nots." And the Church should convince technocrats that a computer, after all, does not have a soul . . . that value judgments come from a renewed spirit, not the number-crunching of statistical chance.

"We either shift upward to a new culture of higher spirituality to turn our electronic technologies into cathedrals of light, or we slide downward to darkness and entropy in a war of each against all."[19]

We must not let the world will its own suicide.

> "The fight, physical and spiritual, for our planet, a fight of cosmic proportions, is not a vague matter of the future; it has already started. The forces of Evil have begun their deci-

sive offensive, you can feel their pressure."[20]

VI. CONCLUSION

16. THE ASSURANCE OF HOPE

Jump Aboard!

Wake up, church! The New Millennium will either midwife God's manifest presence or manifest Satan's maddening malevolence. And this warning doesn't hype one more, forgotten, church-renewal seminar.

History can go either way.

"Yet many church leaders are not aware that the Church—and their church(!)—is facing such a crucial juncture in its history."[1] Far more than a mirror of the "wild west," the future brings a battle for the entire planet's faith. And if we fail to see God's hand in this great event, our punishment will be swift.

Already, churches "risk becoming dinosaurs before the decade is through."[2]

Still, many church leaders remain inert on this whirling earth. They miss how quickly things are moving. Before their day, serious change took as long as two or three generations. In the last twenty-five years, though, major changes have occurred every two to three years.[3] And today, technology outdates itself in days.

In fact, things are moving faster than even extremists can believe. Their wildest predictions are already proving wrong.[4]

And the world has embraced these changes. Like crystal-lized ideas, they are already here . . . irrevocable . . . unstoppable. They are more like vividly shared visions than agreed delusions . . . more like collective births than faddish fantasies. Those who discover this future, for example, speak almost of "conversions." And children suddenly feel more at ease with the new medium than their parents.

The train is moving. Jump aboard!

> "We're seeing signs of a cyber-church emerging. One of the projec-tions we're making is that by the year 2010, between 10 and 20 per-cent of the U.S. population will rely exclusively or primarily on the In-ternet for religious purposes. These people will never set foot on a church campus again."[5]

Letting Go to Lovingly Go

The great advantage of the Church has always been its redemption . . . its own rebirth. So once again, it must release the bondage of the past to rise above the demands of the future.

The Church must die to live.

New breakthroughs come from breaking old rules. New hope derives from dropping old hope. So clergy must discard out-dated language, religious jargon, in-house codes, meaningless metaphors, and archaic styles.

Regardless of their boomer flesh, today's church leaders must turn from hyped spirituality and the needless beliefs, styles, and tics that tick off today's youth. They must scrap all the programs for the sake of programs and all the buildings for the sake of buildings.

No matter the "CEO" clergy, they must move beyond the old world of pushy leaders and passive followers—the one-way, one-to-many style of "pushed" information. They must move beyond worship, for example, that is done "to" or "for" believers instead of "by" believers.

The church must let go of an irrelevant past if it is to lovingly go into the future.

Possibility Machines

If the Church has been waiting for the right moment to create a new world, this is it. The digital shift will set the course for the future, and the ability to effect change is "what will make the future so different from the present."[6]

Of greater import, the model for the future reflects the same model that created the Church in the first place: a new knowledge . . . a new creativity . . . a new community . . . a new freedom . . . and a new empowerment.

And, amazingly, a new faith also reflects original faith: "If bits can represent anything, then a computer is in its very essence an 'anything' machine...a possibility machine."[7] And so is faith. Faith anticipates the yet-to-be. It looks "to things that are unseen" and "perceives" the things hoped for. Then it gives "substance" to its vision.[8]

Indeed, computers in the hands of Christians fulfill prophecy more than computers in the hands of global entrepreneurs.

So the new church is a creative church. We don't have to wait for the future. We can listen to God and create His Church now!

Being What We Will Be

... and it won't be difficult.

The words to the old hymn, "I Love to Tell the Story," will take on new meaning in the New Millennium. For the digital age will empower the storyteller as never before. A new narrative will allow a new "Word," and a new storytelling will allow a new story.

We have yet to grasp the great expressiveness of this new medium. It will immerse us in sensual images that today's arts can only suggest. In truth, these images will be *more real* than reality. Incredibly, we will walk into the story . . . and the story will change.

In this sci-fi world of prophetic art, parsons will be poets, and poets will be parsons. Revivalists will be artists, and artists will be revivalists. So all the church lacks is inspired imagination!

Just as the Creator-God told Moses, "I WILL BE WHAT I WILL BE," the Church—created in His image—"WILL BE WHAT IT WILL BE."

First Steps

Too many possibilities, though, paralyze even sincere souls. But we need not worry about the ascent that lies before us. We can begin with the simplest first steps. Indeed, these simple—yet prayerful—beginnings provide the only impetus we need.

So to get started, simply get curious! Grow open to new ideas . . . become sensitive to projected trends. And, yes, get "on-line," but even more helpful, learn the life-styles—both "on-line" and "off-line"—of the changing scene.

In other words, leave the technology to the technicians and concentrate on the fun things . . . the "big picture" . . . the exciting visions. Technology changes too fast anyway. We can get lost in it. But keeping our eyes on the horizon keeps us securely on course.

(It doesn't hurt, though, to have a technician as a friend!)

Next, begin experimenting . . . trying as many "safe" hunches as possible . . . testing ideas that bring change . . . creating models of the future . . . going *from* somewhere *to* something.

And here are the probable prototypes:

Eggs in Many Baskets

The digital tide rolls in on four potent waves. Negroponte calls them "decentralizing," "empowering," "globalizing," and "harmonizing." So the majority of our tests should ride the crest of these waves.[9]

First, "decentralizing" requires a new polity and a new structure . . . a new way of making decisions and a new way of carrying out decisions. The old top-down, centralized, command-and-control bureaucracies no longer work in the rapidity of real-time reality. And programs for the sake of programs fail for the same reasons.

So we must test new styles for leaders. We must try "horizontal," or relational, leaders in place of "vertical," or command-and-control, leaders. We must study a non-"turf" polity . . . a non-territorial alliance.

In short, we must try putting eggs in many baskets instead of just one.

This transition means our clergy must change from CEO's to servants. They must mentor other leaders more than magnifying their own leadership. They must empower other piety more than pumping up their own empowerment. They must get others to go with their gifts more than growing their own gifts.

In short, they must model more than they maintain. They must relate more than they rule.

> "Being willing to sacrifice power
> and status for the sake of service to
> the gospel will do more for the
> Church's message about Jesus than
> any amount of rhetoric from
> pulpits."[10]

A New Vitality

There are benefits here for both leaders and laity. Leaders find that shared powers expand . . . that significance means more than success . . . that active doers achieve more than passive followers . . . that the "priesthood of all believers" empowers the Church more than the "bureaucracy of all priests."

New Millennium leaders also discover that "small" is not only beautiful, but powerful. For example, "cottage ministries" can publish "on-line" with no paper costs, no printing costs, and no postage costs. And small staffs can broadcast video and sound to the world with no TV station costs.

In the same way, these leaders find that large assets and infrastructures prove liabilities in a fluid and flexible world . . . that decision making free of bureaucratic bottlenecks follows the real-time leading of the Holy Spirit . . . that budgets released from the burdens of large institutions serve new and exciting ministries.

The "led," on the other hand, find their voices speaking also with anointing . . . their missions proving also ordained . . . their gifts becoming also unique. No longer passive bystanders, this new laity finds liberation in teamwork and interaction.

Their vitality, once lost, now is found.

Larger Than Local

Finally, the "decentralizing" trend of the New Millennium implies a new community . . . a *different* community. In the past, "nearness" proved the only basis for friends, teams, neighbors, worship. . . . But all that has changed.

Local is no longer local.

Until now, we had to accept whatever church availed itself . . . whatever dogma was offered . . . and whenever it was offered. Some believers—because of race, culture, or social standing—were even turned away! Today, however, any church hoping to survive must prove open, accessible, inclusive, and diverse enough to include, potentially, the full range of humanity.

So we must test the idea of flexible churches—crossing all barriers of time, space, culture, geography, tradition, and other fleshly things. And, since other faiths already worship "on-line," Christians must network their worship too.

In other words, anything we do locally must be done on behalf of something larger than local. That's what it means to be a "local" success.

Making Us Believe

The second great wave of the future brings an "empowering" theme. Besides a new voice for those without a voice, it brings a new language for those without a language. Indeed, it brings a postmodern language of great evocative power.

And it will change the world.

For the Church, this postmodern language will take the form of endless "prophetic metaphors." A constant flow of fluid and fleeting images will replace our linear and logical rhetoric as the preferred path to religious experience.[11] Because—when prophetic—metaphors create us more that we create them. They inform us more than we inform them. Since they are "active forces in the world," Carl Hausman writes, they bring "things into being."

Even today, the prophetic metaphors of artists "are not so much describing the world as creating a new one."[12]

According to Paul Ricoeur, this metaphor grounds itself "within a Christian vista of promise and hope." It makes the intangible tangible . . . the invisible visible . . . the implicit explicit.

And it "has the power not only to generate meaning but ultimately to change the world."[13]

For the same reasons, Murray Krieger claims it invokes "the miraculous," and Jose Ortega y Gasset calls it "the most fertile power possessed by man."

Yet this power manifests itself without the computer. So consider the two together—prophetic metaphors and the digital realm. Already, a mere click of a button instantly transfers billions of dollars to anywhere in the world. And—like a metaphor—this transfer is not real money. Yet, it somehow "becomes" real money.

It's a make-believe that makes us believe!

In a similar way, digital metaphors can become "real." Their virtual—yet divine—reality can make us believe.

A Privileged Parlance

Long before this postmodern language, the ancient Hebrews spoke through metaphor. Or, more to the point, God spoke to them through metaphor. Then—through prophecy—they shared this vision with others. Finally—and miraculously—their vision went forth and did things.

It "renewed the face of the earth."[14]

Remember the greatest metaphor of all time: Jesus! Spirit became flesh . . . and pointed out of the power to which it pointed. This God/man said, "Anyone who has seen Me has seen the Father."[15] And—like the prophets who acted out their prophetic metaphors—His very life reflected the glory of God. In short, He modeled all the elements of prophetic metaphor.

We, too, are metaphors, for we are "molded in the image of His Son."[16] So our faith also requires learning to speak this ancient/new language.

Trying out these postmodern metaphors, we must first study the practical dynamics of Hosea's prophetic metaphor—the "known," the "unknown," and the "transcendent." Then we must keep our eyes open for visionary trends in the arts, especially movies and alternative music. Finally, we must try our hand with the new "syntax" of cyberspace—hypertext, virtual reality, digital dialogue, implicit images, multimedia, speeding icons, global themes. . . .

And we must do it all in the context of an art. Indeed, art may well become the privileged parlance of the future. But it will speak to us without its usual trappings. Though metaphor represents the very structure of the arts, it has nothing to do with the arts as we define them. Where today's "fine arts" divide into strict classes of music, drama, dance, visual art, and poetry, metaphor knows no such division. And where "high" art sets itself above life itself, metaphor knows no such deity.

And one final warning: Negroponte says any information or entertainment provider who refuses to explore this new language will soon be out of business.[17]

This word of advice applies, as well, to the church.

"You shall receive power (in order
to) be My witnesses."[18]

Breaking the Codes

The third wave of the digital age, "globalization," raises the question of "mission" in an electronic, global community. But to answer this question, we must check our notions.

We must step outside our box.

Then, we will realize the disaster of strict conformity to a *culturally* "religious" code . . . to all the things that have nothing to do with Christianity. Then, we will see among the resources of the church—the Bible, the Holy Spirit, time, space, and believers—that the last four were always flexible. As a result, we will grasp the great need to break barriers.

After all—Martin Luther saw—as long as the gospel is clear, nothing else matters!

So New Millennium evangelism will break the barriers of geography, genre, gender, and generation. It will cross the boundaries separating sacred and secular . . . religious and nonreligious . . . pious and profane . . . clergy and laity . . . church and world . . . familiar and foreign . . . "us" and "them."

It will do this by reaching anyone, anywhere, anytime, anyway. It will try reaching "different"souls in "different" places at "different" times and in "different" ways. And, in the process, it will explore cross-cultural meanings, multicultural expressions, and even counter-cultural idioms.

A Reconciling Resonance

As we fathom the digital future, Negroponte says the fourth wave brings a "harmonizing" sound. In a Christless culture, of course, we hear only disharmony. But there's a reconciling resonance that rings loud and clear for the Church.

Listen.

The Church must take an abused technology and turn it to good. We must show up at the point where God's will and the world's will part ways and unite them with truth. We must name the unjust deeds of the new "supermen" and purge wrongness from their wrongs.

Someday, we must be able to say, they "thought evil against (us), but God meant it for good."[19]

After all, the Church is the only force that can transcend the moment, yet prophetically effect it. We are the only ones who can escape a fallen world, yet heal it. We are the only ones who can avoid the demons of our age, yet respond in love for their victims.

And we find these mandates, first, in the call for "equity" . . . in the claim for equal access to the new technology . . . in the need for "user-friendliness" for every global citizen.

For freedom of information may very well mean freedom for spiritual growth.

We find these mandates, also, in the call for a new "clearing house"—a place where truth is screened from a world of information overload. Someone must value wisdom more than data . . . quality more than quantity . . . validity more than volume.

Someone must separate the wheat from the chaff. Someone must say, "This isn't good."

For in the end, "Data kills, but the Spirit gives life."[20]

Pentecost or Babel?

History sobers us. It suggests that big institutions would rather die than change . . . would rather decline than lose their influence. Current trends also sober us. They suggest that today's youth would rather shape new alliances than accept old ones . . . would rather create new forms than embrace the ones we have.

So, historically, our hope is lost in the middle between history and trends.

But we can't turn back. We can't "just say no" to the new technology . . . to the postmodern world . . . to the young with different dreams. The New Millennium Church faces a new world with new rules.

And everything is at stake!

The fight for our planet is not a vague matter of the future. This cosmic, high-stakes battle has already started. It is a new theater of operations in an ageless war over the human heart. Only this time— someone said—"The next century will be spiritual or it won't be at all."

This book shouts the final call to arms and the final order of the day.

We need a new vision for the Church . . . a greater vision . . . the vision of an astronaut for whom dusk and dawn are a single horizon. We need a new voice for the Church . . . a greater voice . . . the voice of a prophet who "calls those things that be not as though they were."

May the world find torrents of Pentecost within the terrors of this new Babel.

ABOUT THE AUTHOR

Dr. Thomas Hohstadt has achieved recognition in several fields: international symphony conductor, author, lecturer, recording artist, composer, and soloist. A Fulbright scholar, he holds four advanced degrees from the Eastman School of Music and the Vienna *Akademie für Musik*. A twenty-eight-year conducting career includes positions with the Eastman School of Music; the Honolulu, Amarillo, and Midland-Odessa Symphonies; and guest appearances in eight nations.

During this time, Hohstadt also authored two award-winning books and twenty-six articles. A devoted Christian and instructor at the International Worship Institute, he opens new visions of empowered worship through the theology of creativity and the prophetic metaphor. In his book, *Spirit and Emotion*, he cracks the conspiracy of natural emotion posing as spirituality. And in this latest book, *Dying to Live*, Hohstadt combines scholarly skills and prescient insight to explore the new Church of the Digital Age.

Informed writers praise his previous works:

. . . an issue whose 'time has come' . . . of major importance . . . skillful communication." Robert Webber, Director of The Institute for Worship Studies and Professor of Theology, Wheaton College

" . . . the most scholarly, sensible, and scriptural book on the creative power of music I have ever read. . . . a 'must' book for all worshipers." Judson Cornwall, author and lecturer

". . . crammed with insight, unsettling, counter-cultural, yet never fueled by the desire to startle the reader and raise a stir." Grace Mojtabai, former Harvard professor

"A William Blake quality . . . aphoristic . . . like poetry. It ignites things . . . it's provocative . . . it has sentences that blow your mind." Katherine Veninga, Editor, *Texas Journal of Ideas, History and Culture*

"Awesome . . . on to something important . . . a wonderful way with words, often brilliant." Bishop Leroy T. Matthiesen, Diocese of Amarillo

ENDNOTES

INTRODUCTION
1. APOCALYPTIC VISIONS

1. *Time*, Jan 14, 1991, p. 65.

2. Mark 4:22, AMP.

3. Loren B. Mead, *The Once and Future Church* (Bethesda, MD: The Alban Institute, 1991) p. 39.

4. Mark Driscoll, quoted in Sarah Means, "Postmodern Church Targets Generation X in Seattle," *The Washington Times*, http://www.washtimes.com:80/culture/ culture2.html.

5. William Irwin Thompson, *The Time Falling Bodies Take to Light: Mythology, Sexuality, and the Origins of Culture* (New York: St. Martin's Press, 1981) p. 103.

6. Thompson, *Coming Into Being* (New York: St. Martin's Press, 1996) p. 199.

7. Don Tapscott, *The Digital Economy: Promise and Peril in the Age of Networked Intelligence* (New York: McGraw-Hill, 1996) p. 16, 17.

8. eStats, Internet, http://www.emarketer.com/estats/nmsg_users_ future.htm, 1998.

9. Larry King Show, CNN, January 3, 1997, an interview with the editor of *Time* magazine.

10. Reuters News Agency, Internet, http://nt.excite.com/news/r/981117/17/odd-computer, Nov. 17, 1998.

11. Isaiah 43:19, AMP.

12. Michael S. Driscoll, "The Roman Catholic Mass," *The Complete Library of Christian Worship*, Volume two, (Nashville: Star Song Publishing Group, 1994) p. 173.

13. Luke 13:34, AMP.

14. Sally Morgenthaler, *Worship Evangelism* (Grand Rapids: Zondervan Publishing House, 1995) p. 52.

15. Paul L. Maier, in *A Skeleton in God's Closet*.

16. Alvin Toffler, *Creating a New Civilization* (Atlanta: Turner Publishing Company, 1994) p. 35.

17. Harvey Cox, Fire from Heaven: *The Rise of Pentecostal Spirituality and the Reshaping of Religion in the Twenty-first Century* (Reading, Massachusetts: Addison-Wesley Publishing Company, 1995) p. 116.

18. Mead, p. 68.

19. "Using the Internet," Television broadcast, Corporation for Public Broadcasting, 1996.

20. Hebrews 13:8, AMP.

2. HOW WE GOT HERE . . .

1. Some ideas in this chapter and the next find their inspiration in a proposed book by Rex Miller. For further inquiry, write: Rex Miller, 2070 Cobblestone Lane, Reston, Virginia 22091.

2. Matthew 26:26, John 9:6.

3. Romans 4:17, Isaiah 46:10; AMP.

4. I Kings 18:41, AMP.

5. John 16:33, AMP.

6. Carl Hausman, *Metaphor and Art: Interactionism and Reference in the Verbal and Nonverbal Arts* (New York: Cambridge University Press, 1989) pp. 5, 111, 198.

7. Morny Joy, "Images: Images and Imagination," *The Encyclopedia of Religion*, 1987 ed., VII, 108.

8. The different communication media actually overlap each other. When book lovers first started to read, they read aloud. It did not occur to them they could read silently. Doris Lessing says the change to silent reading took two and a half to three centuries. We find similar—though shorter—overlappings in this century.

9. Protestant churches, especially Calvinist as distinguished from Lutheran.

10. Wade Clark Roof, "God is in the details: Reflections on Religion's Public Presence in the United States in the Mid-1990's," a speech to the Association for the Sociology of Religion, Washington, Summer 1996.

11. Rev. David Bell, an Australian visionary.

12. Examples of these "holy spirit revivals" include the American frontier revivals and camp meetings, the Holiness Movement, the Pentecostal Movement, the Latter Rain Movement, the Vineyard Movement, the Toronto Blessing, and the Pensacola Revival.

13. Cox, p.156.

14. C. Peter Wagner, "The New Apostolic Reformation: The Search to Name a Movement," *Ministry Advantage*, Vol. 6, No. 4, July/Aug. 1996 (pub. by Fuller Theological Seminary) p. 4.

15. Roof.

16. Donald E. Miller, "New-Paradigm Churches in the Twentieth Century," *Ministry Advantage*, Vol. 6, No. 4, July/Aug. 1996 (pub. by Fuller Theological Seminary) p. 1-3.

17. Henry Jauhiainen, "A Pentecostal/Charismatic Manifesto," *Twenty Centuries of Christian Worship*, Robert E. Webber, editor, Volume II, p. 337.

18. II Cor 2:17, *The Message Bible*.

3. . . . WHERE WE'RE GOING

1. David Lochhead, *Theology in a Ditigal World* (United Church Publishing House, United Church of Canada, 1988), p. 54.

2. Sarah Means quotes British theologian and author Os Guinness in "Postmodern Church Targets Generation X in Seattle," The Washington Times, http://www.washtimes.com:80/culture/ culture2.html. (Also, Guinness wrote in a letter to me, "Only positive philosophies endure and postmodernism is radically negative. You could not build or sustain a family, a university, or a nation on it, so it simply cannot last." So considering the trends that promise a new and powerful language of the future—what I call prophetic metaphor—we could speak of a "*post*-postmodernism.")

3. "New Age," Internet article, found in alt.culture, http://www.pathfinder.com/altculture/ aentries/n/newxage.html.

4. Jon Katz, "Can Religion Go Interactive?" Internet, August 6, 1998; http://www.hotwired. com:80/synapse/katz/98/31/katz3a_text.html.

5. Psalm 137:4.

6. Alt.culture, Internet, http://www.pathfinder.com/ altculture/aentries/i/internet.html.

II. THE PROMISE
4. "EXCEEDINGLY GREAT PROMISES"

1. Toffler, pp. 12, 21.

2. Cox, p. 301.

3. Charles Arn, "Are Your Paradigms Working For You or Against You?" *Ministry Advantage*, Vol. 6, No. 4, July/Aug. 1996 (Fuller Theological Seminary) p. 9.

4. Rex Miller, unpublished notes.

5. Lochhead, p. 28.

6. Thompson, p. ix.

7. Lochhead, pp. 25, 26.

8. Nicholas Negroponte, *Being Digital* (New York: Alfred A. Knopf, 1995) p. 231.

9. Negroponte, p. 6.

10. Lochhead, p. 30.

11. Ephesians 5:1, II Peter 1:4; AMP.

12. Toffler, pp. 36, 37.

13. Tapscott, pp. 58, 59.

14. Negroponte, pp. 153, 154.

15. Tapscott, pp. 61, 62.

16. Patricia Seabald, "Designing Information Age Organizations," *Paradigm Shift* April 22, 1991.

17. Hebrews 11:1.

18. Negroponte, p. 183.

19. Rex Miller.

20. Negroponte, p. 230.

21. Negroponte, p. 45.

22. Rex Miller.

23. Negroponte, p. 45.

24. Riel Miller, Alliance for Converging Technologies, 1995, quoted in Tapscott, p. 41.

25. Tapscott, p. 234.

26. LaMar Boschman, Lecture at the International Worship Institute, Dallas, Texas, June, 1996.

27. Lochhead, pp. 26, 27.

28. Mead, p. 53.

29. Lochhead, p. 21.

30. Tapscott, p. 91.

31. Negroponte, pp. 229, 230.

32. Toffler, 34.

33. Negroponte, p. 182.

34. James H. Rutz, *The Open Church* (Auburn, Maine: The SeedSowers, 1992) p. 146.

35. Toffler, p. 40.

36. Lochhead, p. 63.

37. Lochhead, p. 15.

38. Rex Miller.

39. Jacques Ellul, *The Technological Bluff* (Grand Rapids: Eerdmans, 1990), pp. 35, 39.

40. Romans 5:20, KJ.

5. "ONCE MORE WITH FEELING"
1. Rex Miller.

2. II Timothy 3:5.

3. Negroponte, p. 221.

4. Lochhead, pp. 18, 19, 59, 63.

5. Negroponte, p. 119.

6. Walt Whitman, "Leaves of Grass" (My brackets).

7. II Corinthians 3:3, my parentheses; AMP.

8. Toffler, pp. 36, 37.

9. Negroponte, p. 60.

10. Numbers 22:21-33.

11. Hausman, p. 231.

12. Tapscott, p. 107.

13. Tapscott.

14. Thompson, *The Time Falling Bodies Take to Light*, p. 4.

15. Lochhead, p. 90.

16. Negroponte, p. 222.

17. Tapscott, pp. 61, 62.

18. Romans 4:17, KJ.

19. Hebrews 11:1

20. Lochhead, p. 24.

21. Negroponte, p. 116.

22. Howard Rheingold, "Douglas Trumball's Big Budger VR," *Wired*, 1.5.

23. I John 4:1, NIV.

24. Romans 1:21, AMP.

25. Negroponte, p. 99.

26. Thompson, p. 260.

27. Toffler, p. 54.

28. Negroponte, pp. 69, 70.

29. Tal Brooke, *Virtual Gods* (Eugene, Oregon: Harvest House Publishers, 1997) p. 100.

30. II Corinthians 3:18, Expanded Bible.

31. Seabald.

32. Tapscott, p. 226.

33. Negroponte, pp. 163-165.

34. Riel Miller, p. 41.

35. Rex Miller.

36. Boschman.

37. Matthew 16:2, 3; AMP.

III. THE IMPERATIVE
6. EATING ELEPHANTS
1. Lochhead, p. 64.

2. A Hebrew proverb.

3. I Chronicles 12:32, AMP.

4. Alexander Solzhenitsyn, *National Review*, July 7, 1978, p. 838.

5. Brooke, p. 119.

6. Rutz, p. 153.

7. Rutz.

8. Rex Miller, unpublished notes.

9. Toffler, 34.

10. Mead, p. 73.

7. DYING TO LIVE
1. Mead, p. 6.

2. Mead, pp. 62, 63.

3. James 1:26, AMP.

4. Morgenthaler, p. 19.

5. Thompson, *The Time Falling Bodies Take to Light*, p. 92.

6. Morgenthaler, p. 104.

7. Jeremiah 7:3-11, 31:31-34.

8. I Corinthians 1:12, *The Message Bible*.

9. I Corinthians 15:31, AMP.

10. International Committee on English in the Liturgy, *Constitution on the Sacred Liturgy*, chapters 1-6; reprinted from *Documents on the Liturgy*, 1963-1979: *Conciliar, Papal, and Curial Texts* (Collegeville, Minn.: Liturgical Press, 1982).

11. I Cor 1:12-24, Matthew 12:1-17; *The Message Bible*, pp. 402, 39.

12. Maier.

8. TURNING THE CHURCH UPSIDE-DOWN
1. Negroponte, p. 229.

2. Hebrews 2:12, AMP.

3. Toffler, 81, 12.

4. Negroponte, p. 229, 230.

5. Rutz, p. 31.

6. Rutz, p. 107.

7. Philippians 2:7.

8. Mead, p. 55.

9. Rex Miller, unpublished notes.

10. Rutz, p. 41.

11. Rutz.

12. I Peter 5:1-3, AMP.

13. Romans 12:2-10 *The Message Bible*.

14. Donald E. Miller, p. 1-3.

15. Acts 2:42-46.

16. I Peter 2:9.

17. I Corinthians 14:26, AMP.

18. Negroponte, pp. 163-165.

19. Tapscott, p. 234.

20. LaMar Boschman, in a lecture at the International Worship Institute, 1997.

21. T. R. Morton, *Knowing Jesus* (Philadelphia: Westminster, 1974).

9. CROSSING FORBIDDEN BORDERS

1. Thompson, *Coming Into Being* p. 261.

2. Morgenthaler, p. 79.

3. Negroponte, p. 165.

4. Matthew 18:20, AMP.

5. John 4:21, 23.

6. Lars Bojen Nielsen," Do God and Cyber-Angels Surf the Net?" Internet, http://www.winet.dk/kunder/kirke/feature/godsrf-e.htm, February 10, 1996.

7. Morgenthaler, p. 235-238.

8. Galatians 3:28.

9. Solzhenitsyn, p. 839.

10. Tapscott, p. xv.

11. Sally Morgenthaler, p. 31.

12. Negroponte, p. 224.

13. Negroponte, pp. 6, 204.

14. Negroponte, p. 231.

15. Tapscott, p. 20.

16. Nielsen.

IV. THE PROPHETIC
10. NEEDING A NEW "WORD"

1. Lochhead, "Technology, Communication and the Future," a lecture at the Ecunet '95 conference, Baltimore, MD, May 24, 1995.

2. John Smith, an Australian church leader, quoted in Morgenthaler, p. 127.

3. Stephen Lawhead, *Arthur* (Grand Rapids: Zondervan Publishing House, 1996) p. 219.

4. Lochhead, *Shifting Realities: Information Technology and the Church* (Geneva: WCC Publications, 1997) p. 97-100.

5. We hear this comment among the "deconstructionists" of radical hermeneutics.

6. Lochhead: "Theology and Interpretation: A Footnote to McLuhan," The Internet: http://www.interchg.ubc.ca/dml/martin.html (This essay was first published in the *Journal of Theology*. Dayton: United Theological Seminary, 1994).

7. Thompson, *Coming Into Being*, p. 135.

8. W. E. Vine, *A Comprehensive Dictionary of the Original Greek Words with their precise Meanings for English Readers* (Peabody, Massachusetts: Hendrickson, 1989) p. 1244.

9. I Thessalonians 2:13; Colossians 2:3; I Corinthians 4:20, 2:1, 4; AMP.

10. David Bell, *The Cyberchurch* (an unpublished book).

11. Mark 2:22.

12. Matthew 7:1-16, *The Message Bible*, p. 27.

13. II Corinthians 2:17, *The Message Bible*, p. 441.

14. I Corinthians 3:1-18, *The Message Bible*, pp.405, 406.

15. Jeremiah 7:3-11, 31:31-34.

16. Thompson, p. 151.

11. REDISCOVERING *DAMAH*
1. Hosea 12:10.

2. Genesis 1:26, AMP.

3. Ezekiel 24:1-3, AMP.

4. Ezekiel 1:28, AMP.

5. Mark 4:30, 34; AMP.

6. Romans 6:5, AMP.

7. I Corinthians 2:9-13, KJ.

8. Typical is the work of Paul Ricoeur. The central themes of this renowned philosopher focus on metaphor and religious language. See Lewis Edwin Hahn, Editor, The Philosophy of Paul Ricoeur (Chicago: Open Court, 1995).

9. II Corinthians 3:3, my parentheses; AMP.

10. Romans 10:17, KJ.

11. OMNI, April, '89, p. 44.

12. Robert E. Webber, *Worship Old & New: A Biblical, Historical, and Practical Introduction* (Revised Edition) (Grand Rapids: Zondervan Publishing House, 1994) p. 29.

13. II Kings 3:11-16, AMP.

14. I Chronicles 25:1, 7; II Chronicles 29:30.

15. Ezekiel 32:33, AMP.

16. Hosea 12:10, AMP.

17. I Kings 2:29-32, Jeremiah 13:1-9, 27:1-7; Ezekiel 4:1-3, 5:1-4.

18. Hausman, p. 231.

19. John 16:29, AMP.

20. I Corinthians 2:14, AMP.

21. Psalm 34:8, KJ.

12. THE DYNAMICS OF *DAMAH*

1. Isaiah 1:18, KJ.

2. Hausman, p. 231.

3. Ecclesiasticus 39:1-5, *Apocrypha*.

4. Hebrews 11:1.

5. Matthew 13:10-17, AMP.

6. Lochhead, *Shifting Realities*, pp. 96, 97.

7. Matthew 5:8; II Timothy 2:22; AMP.

8. I Chronicles 25:1, 7.

9. John 16:29.

10. I Corinthians 14:15.

11. I Corinthians 3:16-17; I Peter 2:9.

12. Frank Burch Brown, *Religious Aesthetics: A Theological Study of Making and Meaning* (Princeton, New Jersey: Princeton University Press, 1989) pp.125, 126.

13. Robert E. Webber, Editor, *The Complete Library of Christian Worship* (Nashville: Star Song Publishing Group, 1994) II, pp. 80-82.

14. Webber, II, p. 86.

15. John 3:6; AMP.

16. I Corinthians 4:20, AMP.

17. I Corinthians 2:4, 13; AMP.

18. II Corinthians 5:17, AMP.

19. Luke 24:30-31, AMP.

20. Psalm 18:2, AMP.

21. II Peter 1:21, I Peter 1:10-12, II Peter 3:16; AMP.

22. Brown, "Characteristics of Art and the Character of Theological Education," *Theological Education*, Volume XXXI, Number 1, Autumn 1994, p. 10.

23. I Corinthians 13:9, KJ.

13. MISCARRIED METAPHORS
1. Cox, p. 116.

2. I Corinthians 14:15, AMP.

3. I Corinthians 12:1, KJ.

4. I Corinthians 14:32, AMP.

5. Isaiah 29:13, AMP.

6. Jeremiah 7:3-11, 31:31-34.

7. II Timothy 3:5, AMP.

8. Martin Luther, *Formula Missae*, published in 1523.

9. Matthew 12:1-17, *The Message Bible* p. 39.

10. Spiros Zodhiates, *The Complete Word Study Dictionary: New Testament* (Chattanooga, TN: AMG Publishers, 1993) p. 1181.

11. Luke 4:16, AMP.

12. John 6:31-33, 48-50, 57, 58.

13. II Corinthians 2:17, *The Message Bible.*

14. Matthew 13:52, AMP.

15. I Thessalonians 2:13, AMP.

16. Romans 8:6, AMP.

17. Hebrews 11:1, KJ and AMP.

18. Psalm 33:3.

19. Exodus 16.

20. Isaiah 43:19, AMP.

21. Romans 12:1, 2; *The Message Bible.*

22. I Corinthians 3:1-18, *The Message Bible.*

V. THE PERIL
14. FEELING OUR WAY

1. "Human Emotion," *The New Encyclopædia Britannica* (Chicago: Encyclopædia Britannica, 1994) 15th Edition, Volume 18, pp. 248-256.

2. Daniel Goleman, *Emotional Intelligence* (New York: Bantam, 1995).

3. Antonio R. Damasio, *Descartes' Error: Emotion, Reason, and the Human Brain* (New York: Grosset/Putnam, 1994) pp. 48, 49, 159, 160, 234.

4. Cox, p. 301.

5. This subject is covered more extensively in my book, *Spirit and Emotion: Beyond the Soul* (1997) available at: Damah Media, 3522 Maple Street, Odessa, Texas 79762.

6. Beginning in John 21:15, the original Greek gives two different words for love: one natural, the other spiritual. Modern translations don't show this.

7. Romans 10:2, AMP.

8. Ephesians 4:22, AMP.

9. Job 15:12, AMP.

10. II Corinthians 10:17.

11. Proverbs 26:12, AMP.

12. Matthew 6:1, 2; AMP.

13. II Timothy 3:5, AMP.

14. Jude 12, AMP.

15. Colossians 2:18, AMP.

16. G. Harder, "Soul," *The New International Dictionary of New Testament Theology,* 1986 ed., II, p. 686.

17. D. M. Lake, "Soul," *The Zondervan Pictorial Encyclopedia of the Bible*, 1976 ed., V, 496.

18. Zodhiates, pp. 1180, 1494. (See also: I Thessalonians 5:23 and Hebrews 4:12.)

19. "Whoever loses his [lower] life (or soul) on My account will find it [the higher life]." Matthew 10:39, AMP.

20. Wisdom XIV:12, *Apocrypha*.

21. Harder, 682-687.

22. Isaiah 50:11, AMP.

23. John 3:6, NIV.

24. I Corinthians 2:14, AMP.

25. Galatians 5:17, AMP.

26. Austin E. Grigg. "Emotion," *Encyclopedia Americana*, 1990 ed., X, p. 309.

27. Grigg, p. 309.

28. Vine, p. 448.

29. Taylor Caldwell, *Great Lion of God* (Garden City, New York: Doubleday & Company, 1970) p. 228, 229.

30. Vine.

31. Zodhiates, p. 1280.

32. I Corinthians 3:3, AMP.

33. Romans 8:13; Ephesians 4:22, 23; AMP.

34. Lamentations 3:22, 23; AMP.

35. I Peter 5:8; AMP.

36. I John 4:1, AMP.

37. I Thessalonians 5:21, AMP.

38. II Corinthians 11:14, 15; AMP.

39. Luke 9:54-56, AMP.

40. James 4:7, AMP.

41. Hosea 4:6, KJ.

42. John 3:6, NIV.

43. E Beyreuther and G. Finkenrath, "Joy," *The New International Dictionary of New Testament Theology*, 1986 ed., II, p. 352.

44. I John 4:7, II Corinthians 8:16, Galatians 5:22; AMP.

45. II Corinthians 7:10, AMP.

46. Romans 5:3, AMP.

47. Galatians 5:6, AMP.

48. Hebrews 11:1, AMP; my parentheses.

49. Revelation 2:23, AMP.

15. DIGITAL DEMONS
1. Lochhead, "Technology, Communication and the Future."

2. Negroponte, pp. 228, 229.

3. Solzhenitsyn, p. 840.

4. Lochhead, *Theology in a Ditigal World*, p. 34.

5. Lochhead, "A Software World," a 1991 lecture, http://www.interchg.ubc.ca/dml/software.html.

6. Brooke, p.35.

7. John Perry Barlow, "Crime and Puzzlement," Internet, 1990, Electronic Frontier Foundation's World Wide Web site, http://www.eff.org.

8. Thompson, *Coming Into Being*, p. 151.

9. Tapscott, pp. 4, 5.

10. Donald L. Maker, "Welcome to the Cyber-Millennium," *Virtual Gods*, Tal Brooke, Editor (Eugene, Oregon; Harvest House Publishers, 1997) p. 44.

11. Brooks Alexander, "Virtuality and Theophobia," *Virtual Gods*, Tal Brooke, Editor (Eugene, Oregon; Harvest House Publishers, 1997) p. 165, 166.

12. Tal Brooke, p. 35.

13. Negroponte, p. 224.

14. Thompson, p. 150.

15. Solzhenitsyn, p. 841.

16. Galations 6:7, KJ.

17. Brooks Alexander, "The Faustian Bargain," *Virtual Gods*, Tal Brooke, Editor (Eugene, Oregon; Harvest House Publishers, 1997) p. 95.

18. Galatians 3:3, NIV.

19. Thompson, p. 9, 10.

20. Solzhenitsyn, p. 840.

VI. CONCLUSION
16. THE ASSURANCE OF HOPE

1. Arn, p. 9.

2. Morgenthaler, p. 136.

3. Seabald.

4. Negroponte, p. 75.

5. David Kinnaman, research director for the Barna Research Group, The Washington Times, Nov. 25, 1989, on-line version.

6. Negroponte, p. 231.

7. Lochhead, pp. 9, 10.

8. Hebrews 11:1.

9. Negroponte, p. 229.

10. Tom Beaudoin, *Virtual Faith*, quoted in "On Media" by Jon Katz. The Internet: http://www.wired.com/news/news/wiredview/story/14277.html.

11. Roof.

12. Thompson, *The Time Falling Bodies Take to Light*, p. 7.

13. Joy, p. 108.

14. Psalm 104:30, NIV.

15. John 14:9, AMP.

16. Romans 8:29, AMP.

17. Negroponte, p. 63.

18. Acts 1:8, AMP.

19. Genesis 15:20, AMP.

20. David Lochhead, quoted by Donald L. Baker in "Welcome to the Cyber-Millennium," *Virtual Gods*, Tal Brooke, Editor, (Eugene, Oregon: Harvest House Publishers, 1997) p. 51.